1066

Martin Co

Series editors: Ma ... • Rosemary Rees

Book 1

Cover image: Celebrating May Day near the town of Riom in the Auvergne. A procession of noble folk, accompanied by musicians, rides out in the woods. By Pol de Limbourg and his brothers, from the manuscript Les Tres Riches Heures du Duc de Berry, 1409–87.

www.heinemann.co.uk

✓ Free online support
✓ Useful weblinks
✓ 24 hour online ordering

01865 888080

Heinemann is an imprint of Pearson Education Limited, a company incorporated in England and Wales, having its registered office at Edinburgh Gate, Harlow, Essex, CM20 2JE. Registered company number: 872828

www.heinemann.co.uk

Heinemann is a registered trademark of Pearson Education Limited

Text © Pearson Education Limited 2008

First published 2008

12 11 10 09 08
10 9 8 7 6 5 4 3 2

British Library Cataloguing in Publication Data is available from the British Library on request.

ISBN 978 0 435318 50 5

Edited by Sandra Stafford
Designed by Ian Lansley
Typesetting and illustration by 𝖳\Tek-Art, Croydon, Surrey
Original illustrations © Pearson Education Ltd 2008
Cover design by David Poole
Picture research by Beatrice Ray
Cover photo/illustration © Mary Evans
Printed in China (SWTC/02)

The author and publisher would like to thank Guardian News and Media Ltd for permission to reproduce an extract from an article by Maev Kennedy that appeared in the Guardian newspaper.

They would also like to thank the following individuals and organisations for permission to reproduce photographs:

AKG: 40A, 146B, 153B; Alamy: 40B, 74A, 86A, 94A, 108A, 110A, 153A, 162A, 162B; Alan Sorrell: 15B; Bodleian Library Oxford: 158A, 170A, 170B, 170C; Bridgeman Art Library: 20A, 22A, 29B, 31A, 50A, 56A, 58C, 58E, 58F, 90A, 104B, 106A, 114A, 115B, 120A, 142B, 145A, 148A, 149C, 157B 166B; British Library: 13A, 42A, 42B, 76A, 76B, 76C, 76D, 98A, 98B, 98C, 127C, 160A, 178A; Bunn/Bridgman Art Library: 27B; Camera Press: 58A; Canterbury Archaeological Trust: 75B; Corbis: 58B, 137A, 153D; Heritage Image Partnership 104A; Fielding/Alamy: 92A; Krause, Johansen/Archivo Iconographico, SA/Corbis: 174A; Lebrecht Music & Arts Photo Library/Alamy 116A; Mary Evans: 157B; Mary Evans Picture Library/Alamy 100B; National Library of Wales: 33A; National Portrait Gallery: 58D; Scala: 157A; Sheridan/ Ancient Art and Architecture:10A, 13B, 15A; Sonia Halliday: 128A; St Edmundsbury Borough Council: 74A; The College of Arms, London: 166A, 168A; The Gallery Collection/Corbis: 63A; Topham Picturepoint: 100A; Victoria and Albert Museum: 84A, 84B; Walker Art Gallery, National Museums Liverpool: 52A.

Every effort has been made to contact copyright holders of material reproduced in this book. Any omissions will be rectified in subsequent printings if notice is given to the publishers.

Websites
There are links to relevant websites in this book. In order to ensure that the links are up to date, that the links work, and that the sites are not inadvertently linked to sites that could be considered offensive, we have made the links available on the Heinemann website at www.heinemann.co.uk/hotlinks. When you access the site, the express code is 8543T.

Contents

Finding out about history

This book has been written to bring your Key Stage 3 History lessons alive and to make sure you get the most out of them! The book is divided into three sections: **Ruling, Living and working** and **Moving and travelling**.

By looking at each of these big themes, you will build up a picture of what life was like for people living in the period 1066 to 1603. You will also be able to find out how life changed and what happened during this period that affected the way people lived and worked, moved around, ruled and were ruled.

You'll not only find out about life in England at this time, but how England got on with its neighbours, Wales and Scotland. You'll also discover what life was like in different parts of the world, such as China, and where people went exploring and why.

Doing history!

In each section of this book there are activities to help you get the most out of that topic. Most sections will have four different types of task, though some will just have the first three:

1. Everyone should be able to have a go at this task.

2. Next, have a go at this task.

3. Once you've completed the blue task, see if you can try this.

4. If you want to stretch yourself, you can have a go at this.

History detective
There will be chances for you to investigate topics in more detail and carry out your own investigations.

Back to the start
You will also be able to review and reflect on the bigger picture and on your own learning.

Practising historical skills

At the end of the book, you'll find a Skills bank. This is to remind you of some of the important historical skills you'll be learning. Use this section for useful hints and tips as you complete the tasks and the activities throughout the book.

Introduction

There were different groups of people living in England in the period 1066–1603. Some people, the very few, were powerful. Most people had little or no power. **Sources a–f** show some pictures of people from the period you are going to study.

Describe what you can see in each picture in as much detail as possible.

A painting from c.1100.

Illustration from a fourteenth-century chronicle.

Image from a manuscript, 1380.

Timeline 1066 –1603

King Edward the Confessor dies — 1066

1066 — Battle of Hastings

The Harrying of the North — 1069

1086 — The Domesday Book

William I dies — 1087

1154 — Henry II becomes king

Murder of Thomas Becket — 1170

1199 — John becomes king

John signs the Magna Carta — 1215

1258 — The Great Council meets

Each picture shows a different type of person who lived in the period 1066–1603. Match each one to the description below.

(i) Knights: I serve the noble by fighting in his army.

(ii) Merchant: I sell cloth but do not have much power.

(iii) Bishop: the Church has a lot of power and I am an important member of the Church.

(vi) Peasant: I work the land for the noble and have no power.

(iv) King: I am the ruler of the country.

(v) Noble: I swear to serve the king who relies on me for support.

Now, working in pairs, put the people in order of power from the most powerful to the least powerful.

When you have finished your list, compare it with another pair.

Look at the timeline on these pages. It includes some important events from the period that you will be studying. The events are about monarchs, battles (which involve nobles and knights), archbishops and the Church, and peasants. Can you identify which events might involve which types of people?

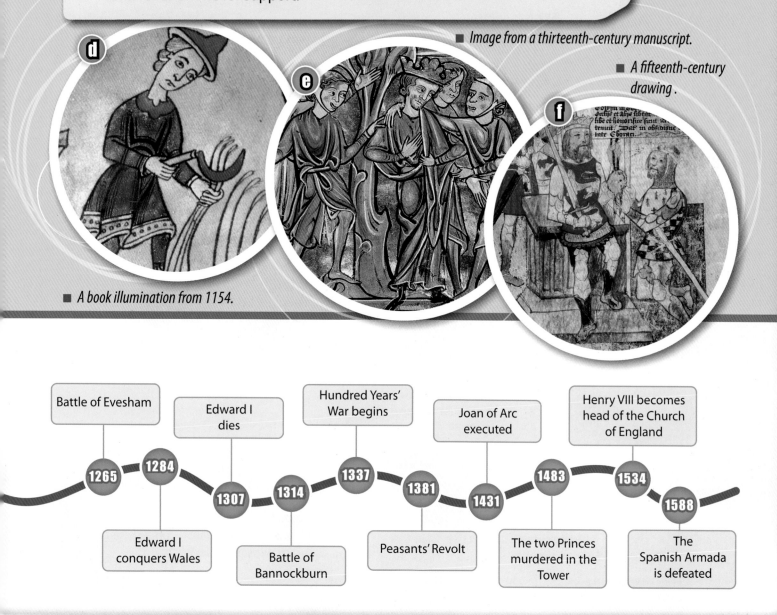

■ *Image from a thirteenth-century manuscript.*

■ *A fifteenth-century drawing .*

■ *A book illumination from 1154.*

Battle of Evesham — **1265**

Edward I dies — **1284**

Edward I conquers Wales — **1307**

Battle of Bannockburn — **1314**

Hundred Years' War begins — **1337**

Peasants' Revolt — **1381**

Joan of Arc executed — **1431**

The two Princes murdered in the Tower — **1483**

Henry VIII becomes head of the Church of England — **1534**

The Spanish Armada is defeated — **1588**

1.1a

In this lesson you will:

■ **find out why people travelled to England**

■ **use maps in your investigation.**

Why go to England?

For hundreds of years up to the eleventh century people risked crossing the seas to get to England. The information on the maps below gives us clues as to why this happened.

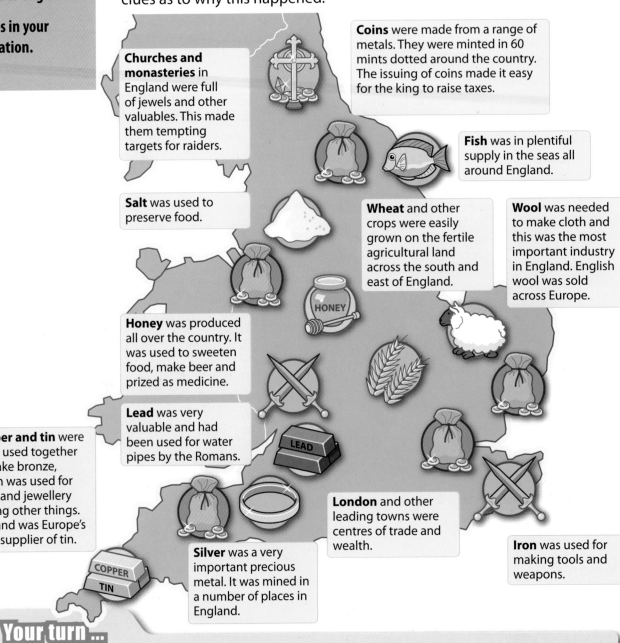

Churches and monasteries in England were full of jewels and other valuables. This made them tempting targets for raiders.

Coins were made from a range of metals. They were minted in 60 mints dotted around the country. The issuing of coins made it easy for the king to raise taxes.

Fish was in plentiful supply in the seas all around England.

Salt was used to preserve food.

Wheat and other crops were easily grown on the fertile agricultural land across the south and east of England.

Wool was needed to make cloth and this was the most important industry in England. English wool was sold across Europe.

Honey was produced all over the country. It was used to sweeten food, make beer and prized as medicine.

Lead was very valuable and had been used for water pipes by the Romans.

Copper and tin were often used together to make bronze, which was used for tools and jewellery among other things. England was Europe's chief supplier of tin.

London and other leading towns were centres of trade and wealth.

Iron was used for making tools and weapons.

Silver was a very important precious metal. It was mined in a number of places in England.

Your turn...

1 a) Look at the map above. Discuss with your group the reasons why people were drawn to England. Put four of the reasons on a spider diagram and explain why they were so attractive. Give this spider diagram the title 'Pull'.

b) Now look at the map on the opposite page, which gives the reasons why people were pushed to go to England. Put three of these reasons on a spider diagram with the title 'Push'.

Vikings

We have travelled the seas for some time trading goods. From around AD 850 onwards we have needed to find places where some of us can settle. There are more and more people in Denmark and Norway and not enough land.

Saxons

Our homes and fields are being flooded by rising sea levels. We need to find a new home. Some of our menfolk have been invited to go to England to help the English fight against the Vikings. They have sent messages back that it is a very nice place.

Normans

We came to Normandy from the north. Our neighbours, the Franks, do not like us. We are looking to conquer other countries to give ourselves greater wealth and security.

Raiders, settlers and conquerors

People came to England for different reasons.

- **Raiders** came to raid England. This meant that they would come, kill whoever stood in their way, take whatever they could and return home.

- **Settlers** came to England to live and work there.

- **Conquerors** came not only to live in England but to conquer and rule the country.

Over to you ...

2 Give reasons why the following groups came to England.

- Saxons
- Vikings
- Normans

In conclusion ...

3 Why did people come to England?

Use the information on these pages to answer the question. List your reasons in order of priority with the first reason being the most important one. You will need to ask yourself the following questions before completing your answer.

- Why were people drawn to England?

- What factors pushed people?

- Which of these factors in your opinion is the most important reason why people came to England?

In this lesson you will:

■ find out what happened at the Battle of Hastings in 1066

■ use sources and information to tell a story.

History detective

Find out as much as you can about the Bayeux Tapestry. You might want to answer these questions.

● When was it made?

● Who made it?

● What story did it tell?

Battle 1066!

On 14 October 1066, the army of the English king, Harold, fought at Hastings against the army of Norman invaders led by Duke William of Normandy. It was to be one of the most important battles in English history.

Background to the battle

In 1065 the English king, Edward the Confessor, died without an obvious heir. William invaded England because he thought Edward had promised he would be the next king. But Harold had other ideas and had already been crowned.

Telling a story

History is often told by the winners of battles or fights rather than the losers. Several people told the story of the Battle of Hastings. Some had been there, but many had not. **Source a** is an extract from the most famous story, the Bayeux Tapestry. The tapestry was made on the instructions of the Normans and finished in 1077.

? *What can you see happening?*

? *Which group of people do you think are the Normans and why?*

■ *Extract from the Bayeux Tapestry, made in the eleventh century.*

What happened at Hastings?

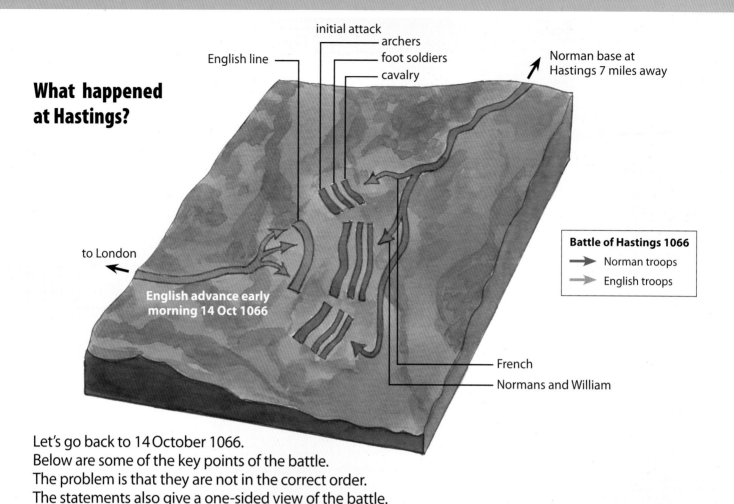

initial attack

archers

foot soldiers

cavalry

English line

Norman base at Hastings 7 miles away

to London

English advance early morning 14 Oct 1066

Battle of Hastings 1066
→ Norman troops
→ English troops

French

Normans and William

Let's go back to 14 October 1066.
Below are some of the key points of the battle.
The problem is that they are not in the correct order.
The statements also give a one-sided view of the battle.

A The two armies started shouting rude things at each other. Then a brave young Norman called Tallifer charged out from the Norman lines towards the English. Brave Tallifer was cut down and killed. The battle had begun.

B On 25 September King Harold defeated a Viking invasion force led by Harald Hardrada at the Battle of Stamford Bridge.

C In the first part of the battle the Norman archers and cavalry didn't make much impact. It seemed as if William was missing but the great leader took off his helmet to show his troops that he was still alive.

D On the evening of 13 October Harold made the stupid decision to fight the battle on Senlac Hill. He placed his army on the high ground, but the position was not suitable for open battle.

E With many of the English army killed on the slopes of Senlac Hill the fight moved closer to Harold's position. The fearless Normans advanced up the hill and Harold was killed. The battle was over.

F As the sun rose on the morning of the 14 October William's army prepared for battle. William placed his archers at the front, foot soldiers behind and the cavalry to the rear.

G William landed with his army at Pevensey on 28 September to rightfully claim his throne.

H Harold's army arrived on the south coast throughout the day on 13 October but his soldiers were tired. By early evening only 7,500 had arrived.

I After showing he was alive, William played a cunning trick. The Normans pretended to run away. The silly English fell for the trick and ran down the hill. The Normans then turned and cut them down.

Your turn ...

1 Read through the statements **A-I**.

a) The writer of these statements is clearly in favour of one side. Which side is it?

b) Make a list of the words that show the author favours one side.

Write a clear account ...

2 Put the events **(A-I)** into chronological order. Then use your time order to write the story of the Battle of Hastings. You can do this in **one** of the following ways:

● as an English soldier

● as a Norman knight

● as an observer who does not belong to either side.

Make your choice and get writing!

Another account of the Battle of Hastings has been left by a Norman called William of Poitiers. The Factfile gives some information about him.

? *What is there in this Factfile that suggests that William of Poitiers may have written a one-sided story in favour of the Normans?*

Factfile

Name
William of Poitiers

Born
Around 1020
in Normandy

Jobs
Knight, soldier, priest and from 1066 chaplain (personal priest) to William, Duke of Normandy

Publications
The Deeds of William, Duke of the Normans, published in 1073

Whose story is he telling?

3 **Sources b–d** are extracts from William of Poitiers' account of part of the battle. Remember, William of Poitiers was probably present at the battle but he was a Norman. Some of the words that William of Poitiers uses in these extracts show he was a Norman. What image of William the Conqueror does he describe?

b *In the front Duke William put foot soldiers armed with arrows and crossbows. In the second rank came the more heavily armed foot soldiers. Lastly came the group of knights. William rode among them showing great courage.*

c *William was a noble general, inspiring courage, sharing danger, more often commanding men to follow than urging them on from the rear.*

d *Now as the day ended the English army realised beyond doubt they could no longer stand against the Normans. They knew they had suffered heavy losses; that Harold himself was dead; they saw the Normans, with not many dead or injured, threatening them more keenly than in the beginning, as if they had found new strength in the fight; they saw that fury of the duke who spared no one who resisted him; they saw that courage which could only find rest in victory. Therefore the English ran away.*

■ *Extracts from William of Poitiers'* The Deeds of William, Duke of the Normans, *published in 1073.*

Back to the start

You have learned a number of things in this enquiry.

● Which part of the enquiry did you find most interesting and why?

● What would you like to find out more about and why?

1.1c Taking it further!

How did Harold die?

As you will have discovered, the Battle of Hastings ended with Harold being killed. **Sources a–d** give different versions of his death. First, look at **sources a** and **b**. Then read **sources c** and **d**.

? *What do they show you about how Harold died?*

a

b

■ Taken from the Bayeux Tapestry, showing Harold's death, eleventh century.

■ William stabbing Harold at the Battle of Hastings, from an English chronicle, c.1280–1300.

c

The first [knight] hit Harold's breast through his shield with the point of his sword causing blood to gush out. The second knight sliced off Harold's head below the protection of the helmet and the third knight pierced the inwards of his belly with his lance. The fourth knight cut off Harold's leg at the thigh.

■ Written by William of Jumièges in 1070. He suggested that Harold was killed by four knights.

d

The battle went one way then the other as long as Harold lived. But when his brain was pierced by an arrow and he fell, the English ran away. One of the Norman knights hacked at Harold's thigh with a sword as he lay on the ground.

■ Written by William of Malmesbury in about 1125.

Work it out!

We want to find out how Harold died. The problem is, some of the sources agree and some differ.

1 Decide which sources agree and which differ.

  a) First, copy and complete a table like this one.

Source a	Source b	Source c	Source d
tells us …	tells us …	tells us …	tells us …

  b) Next, highlight the points on which the sources agree and disagree.

2 Now we need to ask a few questions about the authors of **sources c** and **d**. What questions should we be asking? Here is one to start you off: *Was the author at the battle?* Think of at least two more questions to ask.

3 Consider **sources a–d**. Which source do you trust most and why? Explain your answer as fully as you can.

Next Lesson

In this lesson you will:

- find out why William built castles

- think about why some English cooperated with the Normans and how others might have attacked a Norman castle.

Control by castle!

By the time King William I died in 1087 the Normans had built hundreds of castles across England. Why do you think this was? Remember, William had landed in the south-east of England and had defeated the English King Harold in 1066 in one battle close to the south coast. But that didn't mean that the rest of England would fall meekly in line behind the Normans.

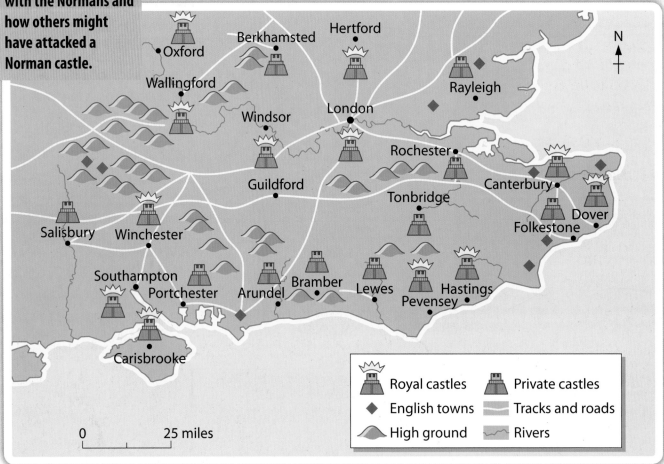

This map shows where the Normans built castles in south-east England during the first ten years of William's reign.

Your turn...

1 Look carefully at the map above.

a) Working with a partner, make lists of the castles that were guarding:
- river crossings
- the coast
- crossroads
- gaps between hills
- English towns.

b) Which castles appear more than once on your list?

c) How many castles are royal castles and how many are private ones?

Over to you...

2 a) What does the map tell you about the reasons why the Normans built castles?

b) Using the map and the information above it, are you surprised that so many castles were built in this part of England? Discuss this with a partner or the rest of your class.

What were William's castles for?

Once outside the reasonably secure south-east corner, the main reason the Normans built castles was to show the English that they were now in charge. A Norman castle was the base from which Norman knights could ride out to end any trouble started by the local people. The larger castles became homes for the new Norman barons and their headquarters for ruling the surrounding countryside.

How were William's castles built?

The Normans brought the first wooden castles with them in sections so that they could be put up quickly. After 1066, the Normans made the English do all the hard work, clearing land to build castles. A Norman castle had to be built where it could command a good view over the surrounding countryside. If anything was in the way, it had to go!

? *Why might the English have co-operated with the Normans?*

■ *Part of the Bayeux Tapestry, eleventh century, showing the Normans building their first castle at Hastings.*

What did William's castles look like?

Motte

Bailey

Ditch

Buildings: kitchen, storeroom, workshops, etc.

Wooden palisade

■ *Alan Sorrell, a present-day artist, did a lot of research and drew this picture to show what he thought the first Norman castles would have looked like.*

Now try this

3 You are one of the English who didn't want to co-operate with the Normans! Use **sources a** and **b** to plan an attack on a Norman castle with your band of freedom fighters. To get you started, here are some things to think about.

● What are the castle's weak points?
● How can you get to them?
● How will you take advantage of them?
● How can you make sure the Norman soldiers don't pour out of the castle and wipe you out?

Remember, there are only about 30 of you and many more Normans.

1.2b

In this lesson you will:

■ find out how William used terror to subdue the English

■ work with sources to decide how accurate this is likely to be.

Terror!

a

There was such hunger that men ate human flesh, and the flesh of horses and dogs and cats. Others sold themselves into slavery so that they could live out their miserable lives. It was horrible to look into the ruined farmyards and houses and see the rotting human corpses, for there were none to bury them for all were gone, either in flight, or cut down by the sword and famine. None lived there and travellers passed in great fear of wild beasts and savage robbers. There was no village inhabited between York and Durham.

■ *Written by Simeon of Durham in the 1100s.*

Think about it...

1 What has happened in **source a**? Clearly something pretty grim.

   a) List what happened to the people.

   b) What clues are there in this extract as to why these terrible things happened?

Source a was written about the north-east of England. But the author only hints at the reason for the terrible devastation.

Why did something terrible happen in the north-east of England?

A The rebellion spread to York, where the English attacked the Norman garrison there.

B William gave much of northern England to the Norman Earl Robert of Commines.

C In September 1069 a Viking army arrived in a fleet of 240 ships and marched to York to support the English rebels.

D Just three years after his invasion, rebels had killed around 1,000 Normans – about one-fifth of the invasion force.

E In January 1069 English rebels surrounded the city of Durham and killed Earl Robert along with about 600 Normans.

F The English and Vikings attacked York castle, made off with its treasure and killed several hundreds of Normans.

Write the story

2 **a)** Read through statements **A–F** and put them in chronological order.

   b) Now use them to write a paragraph explaining why William thought he had to teach the north-east a lesson the people there would not forget.

What did William do?

We know that in 1069 William marched north, determined to secure his kingdom and put an end to any thought of rebellion. But what exactly did he do?
To find out, we have to rely on just a few written sources.

The king stopped at nothing to hunt his enemies. He cut down many people and destroyed homes and land. Nowhere else had he shown such cruelty. He made no attempt to control his fury and he punished the innocent along with the guilty. He ordered crops and herds, tools and food to be burnt to ashes. More than 100,000 people perished from hunger. I have often praised William but I can say nothing good about this brutal slaughter.

■ *Extract from Orderic Vitalis' The Ecclesiastical History, written between 1123 and 1141. Oderic was a monk who had an English mother and a Norman father. This is what he had to say about William's actions.*

Can we trust the evidence?

2 c) Carefully read **sources a** and **b**. Simeon of Durham and Orderic Vitalis make some comments that are the same and some that are very different. On what points do they agree about what happened in the north-east? Write down two/three points.
Set them out like this, then answer the questions on the right.

Simeon and Orderic agree that …

- What does Simeon tell us that Orderic doesn't?
- What does Orderic tell us that Simeon doesn't?
- Are you surprised that Orderic seems to be criticising William?
- Do you think **sources a** and **b** are telling the truth? If not, which do you think is more truthful! Explain your answer.

I fell on the English of the northern shires like a fearsome lion. I ordered their houses and corn, with their tools and goods, to be burnt. I ordered large herds of cattle to be butchered where they were found. By doing so, alas, I became the murderer of many thousands of people, both young and old, of that fine race of people.

■ *Extract from Orderic Vitalis' The Ecclesiastical History, written between 1123 and 1141. This is what Orderic wrote about what William said.*

In conclusion …

3 Does William's confession mean that Simeon of Durham and Orderic Vitalis were right in what they said about William's actions in the north-east of England? Make sure you back up your answer.

Back to the start

William used terror to try to control the English, but how sensible do you think this was and why?

Taking control peacefully

William realised he couldn't hold England by sheer force in the long term. So he developed a cunning plan. He said that all the land was his, but that other people could help him manage it as long as they promised to support him. This was called the feudal system. The diagram on this page shows how it worked.

a

So very narrowly did he [William] have it investigated that there was no single hide nor yard of land, nor, indeed, one ox or cow or pig which was left out and not put down in his record.

■ *From the* Anglo-Saxon Chronicle.

What did William own?

For the feudal system to work, William had to know what sort of a place England was. In 1085, he decided to find out. He sent teams of Norman investigators into the towns and countryside to find out who owned what, and what it was worth. It is not very likely that every cow and pig was counted! But certainly the author of **source a** was anxious to show how thorough William was being.

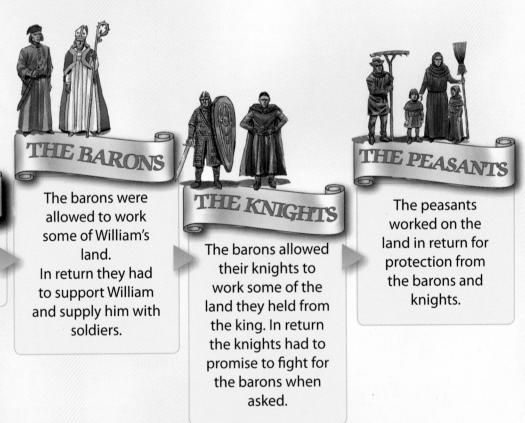

THE KING

William said that all the land in England was his.

THE BARONS

The barons were allowed to work some of William's land.
In return they had to support William and supply him with soldiers.

THE KNIGHTS

The barons allowed their knights to work some of the land they held from the king. In return the knights had to promise to fight for the barons when asked.

THE PEASANTS

The peasants worked on the land in return for protection from the barons and knights.

Everything they recorded was written down in what become known as the Domesday Book. A translation of one section from the Domesday Book is at the top of the next page.

The Land of St Peter of Westminster

*In the vill in which St Peter's Church is situated, the abbot holds 13½ hides. There is land for 11 ploughs. To the **demesne** belongs 9 **hides** and 1 **virgate**, and there are 4 ploughs. The peasants have six ploughs, and there could be 1 plough more. There are 9 **villeins** each on 1 virgate and 1 villein on 1 hide, and 9 villeins on each half a virgate and 1 cottar on 5 acres, and 41 cottars who pay 40 shillings a year for their gardens. Meadow for 11 ploughs, pasture for the livestock of the vill, woodland for 100 pigs, and 25 houses for the abbot's knights and other men who pay 8 shillings a year. In all, it is worth £10 a year.*

Demesne
Land belonging to a lord.
Hide
120 acres of land.
Virgate
30 acres of land.
Villein
Someone who is owned by a feudal lord and has to work for his or her lord.

It's still a bit tricky to understand, isn't it? Try this translation of the entry for Bradford, which was then a manor in Yorkshire.

*In Bradford with six **berewicks**, Gamel had 15 ploughlands for **geld** where may be 8 ploughs. Ilbert has it and it is waste.*

Berewick
An outlying farm.
Geld
A tax levied on land.

Work it out!

1   You might not know the meaning of some of the words, but even without knowing what they mean, which place is the richest and most prosperous? How can you tell?

2   Can you suggest why the Domesday entry for Bradford says 'it is waste'? Hint: find out where Bradford is in England.

3   Make a list of the words in the Domesday entry you don't know, and look them up in a good dictionary. Now write out the entries in modern English so that everyone will understand what they mean.

4   You have looked at three methods William I used to take control of England. Which one do you think was the most successful?

History detective

Find out the answers to these questions.

1   The Normans spoke French and the Anglo-Saxons spoke English. So why was the Domesday Book written in Latin?

2   Why was the Domesday Book called 'Domesday'? Who gave it its name?

Next Lesson

Who had the power: the Crown or the Church?

In this lesson you will:

- work with primary source material to find out how Thomas Becket was murdered

- think about the best ways of communicating information in the twelth century.

Murder in the cathedral

On 29 December 1170 Thomas Becket, the Archbishop of Canterbury, was murdered in his own cathedral. How did this happen?

■ *The murder of Thomas Becket, painted in the 1200s.*

Use your eyes!

1 Look carefully at **source a**. It was painted in the 1200s to show how Thomas Becket was killed. It looks pretty nasty. What's that on the floor? Is it a hat? Is it the top of someone's head ?

Work with a partner and write down two questions you would want to ask about the source to help you understand what is happening in the picture.

What does the written source material say?

Edward Grim wrote **source b**, an account of Thomas Becket's murder. Grim was a priest who was with Becket when he was killed. Read it through carefully.

The murderers arrived in full armour with swords and axes. The monks begged the Archbishop to hide in the cathedral for his own safety, but he refused. This was because he had wanted to be a **martyr** for a long time. However, the monks took no notice of him, seized him and bundled him into the cathedral, bolting the doors behind them. Then Becket said, 'It is wrong to make the house of prayer into a fortress', and he ordered the doors to be kept open.

The knights, following with rapid steps, shouted, 'Where is Archbishop Thomas Becket, a traitor to his king and his country?'

Becket answered, 'I am here. I am a priest of God, not a traitor. I will not run from your swords.'

The knights tried to drag Becket from the Cathedral, but he clung to a pillar, bending his head as if in prayer. One of the knights, Reginald Fitzurse, struck him on his head. He received a second blow to the head, but stood firm. At the third blow he fell to his knees and whispered: 'In the name of Jesus, I am ready to die.' The next blow sliced off the top of his head, and the stone floor was stained with blood white with brain, and with brain red with blood. The fourth knight stopped anyone from interfering with what they were doing. The fifth knight put his foot on Becket's neck. With the tip of his sword he scattered the rest of Becket's brains over the floor and shouted to the others: 'Let's go. This fellow will not be getting up again!'

■ *Written by Edward Grim in the 1170s.*

Compare the sources

2 **a)** Copy this table and fill in as many boxes as you can. You will need to use **sources a** and **b**.

	Source a	Source b
Where did the murder happen?		
How many knights were here?		
What was Thomas Becket doing when he was first struck?		
How many blows were struck?		
Was Becket afraid to die?		
Did Becket want to die?		

b) Which source has given you the most information?

c) Which source do you think is the most interesting? Why?

d) Which source do you think was best for telling people at the time how Thomas Becket was murdered?

Tell the story!

3 What a fantastic story – a king ordering the murder of his archbishop! You want to let as many people as possible know what has happened. But how are you going to do this?

Luckily your uncle is taking a flock of sheep to sell in the market at Northampton. You will go with him. You are planning to stand under the great cross in All Saints Churchyard and shout loudly about the king and Thomas Becket, to attract a crowd.

Planning ahead

● What will be your first 'shout' to make people listen to you?

● Once a crowd has gathered, what will you say to make your story exciting enough to keep them listening?

● Will you be on Becket's side or the king's?

● How will you end your story? What will you try to persuade the crowd to do?

Write it all down – and then try it out on your class!

In this lesson you will:

- **find out why Thomas Becket was murdered**

- **understand that events have long- and short-term causes.**

Key words

Baron
An important landowner who provided men to fight for the king if necessary.

Chancellor
The king's chief minister and adviser.

Repentance
Showing sorrow for something you have done in the past.

Why was Thomas Becket murdered?

You know, from Lesson 1.3a, *how* Thomas Becket was murdered.
But you don't yet know *why* he was murdered.
Perhaps **source a** will give you a clue. It was painted in about 1235.

■ *King Henry II and Thomas Becket arguing, painted c.1235.*

Clues from the picture

1   **Source a** shows King Henry II and his Archbishop, Thomas Becket, quarrelling.

   a) Make a list of the things that tell you they are quarrelling.

   b) Does anything about this picture surprise you?

Friends for ever?

We all have quarrels, but we don't end up murdering the person with whom we have quarreled. So what was the issue between King Henry II and Thomas Becket?

When Henry became king in 1154, he made Becket his **chancellor**. The two men worked well together to make the country strong and prosperous. They became good friends. One of the important things they did together was set up a system of justice. Henry appointed sheriffs and travelling judges, often acting as a judge himself. This meant that the king's justice was respected throughout the land, and the **barons** could no longer run unfair courts. However,

there was a parallel system of justice that Henry couldn't touch: the Church system.

Monks and priests could be tried in Church courts, which often gave more moderate verdicts than the king's courts. Henry wasn't at all happy, either, with the influence the Catholic Church had in England. Bishops were powerful landlords who controlled thousands of acres of land as well as the people who lived here. Yet Henry didn't have a say in appointing bishops in England. This was all done by the Pope in Rome.

Then Henry had a good idea, and that is where the trouble began.

The slippery slope to murder

As soon as Thomas was back in England he broke his promise to Henry. He expelled from the Church all the bishops who had supported Henry while he was away.

In 1161, Henry asked Thomas Becket to be the new Archbishop of Canterbury. Thomas tried hard to persuade Henry that this was a bad idea, but in the end he gave in. Henry's cunning plan was that, with Thomas as Archbishop of Canterbury, the Church could be brought more under Henry's control.

When Henry heard what Thomas had done, he flew into a rage. 'Will no one rid me of this troublesome priest?' he shouted. Some knights heard this and slipped away to do just that.

Henry got a big shock! Instead of serving him, Thomas began serving a new master – God. He began to live a religious life and gave up his rich lifestyle.

Henry passed a law saying that all serious Church court cases had to be tried again and sentenced in the king's courts. Thomas refused to accept this and, in the face of Henry's fury, fled to France.

In July 1170 Henry and Thomas decided to patch up their quarrel. Thomas agreed to come back to England and promised to work under Henry. Henry, satisfied, went to Normandy, to look after his lands there.

Henry decided to show Thomas he could do without him. He had his son crowned as the next king of England by the Archbishop of York. Thomas was very angry: how dare Henry use the wrong archbishop!

Henry was told that the knights had gone. He realised what they were going to do, and was horrified. Desperately, he tried to stop them. But it was too late.

Eight steps to murder

2
a) Put the eight steps to murder in the right order on the slippery slope.
b) What does the story of Thomas Becket's murder tell you about who had the most power in England: the Crown or the Church?
c) Think about the reasons why Becket was murdered. Work with a partner to sort these into long- and short-term causes.
d) Which cause do you think was most important and why? Do others in your class agree?

In conclusion ...

3 You have been asked to write a report for the Lord Chief Justice of England. He wants to know who is to blame for the murder of Thomas Becket. In your report, make it clear whether you think it is King Henry II, the knights or Thomas Becket himself. Remember to back up your opinion with evidence.

Was Henry pleased?

No, he was not! When Henry heard what had happened to Thomas, he was very upset. In 1174 he went to Canterbury, determined to show to everyone his deep sadness at his part in Thomas' murder. Henry, the King of England, walked slowly, barefoot, through the streets of Canterbury to Thomas Becket's tomb. Bishops and monks whipped his back as he passed. Henry, the most powerful king in Europe, was showing his **repentance** and ending his long quarrel with the Church.

 Back to the start

What does the story of the murder of Thomas Becket tell you about who had the most power in England: the Crown or the Church?

In this lesson you will:

- make connections between rights and responsibilities

- reflect on rights and responsibilities under the feudal system.

Rights and responsibilities

If you ruled the world, just for one day, what would you do? What one change would you bring in? Would you feed the world's starving children, or allow free speech in every country or stop the rain forests from being cut down? Or would you stop whale hunting or the development of Antarctica? Of course, you can't rule the world – even for a day. But have you ever wanted to change things in your school?

Teachers shouldn't be allowed to shout at us.

The toilets are disgusting. They should be pulled down and rebuilt.

No one should have to do more than one hour's homework a night.

We should be allowed to design our own school uniform.

We should have more choice of food at school dinners.

Your turn ...

1 In small groups or with a partner think about the things you would like to change in your school. Make a list and share that list with the rest of your class.

What about responsibilities?

If you think you have a right to something you have to think, too, of responsibilities. For example, you have a right to free speech. But you must use this right responsibly. You cannot just say what you think about a person or an event, regardless of whether what you say is true or not. You must make sure that you use the right to free speech responsibly, that what you say is true. You may think you have a right to roam wherever you want to over the countryside. But you must use this right responsibly. You must not walk through fields of standing corn or leave gates open so that animals stray.

Over to you ...

2 Look carefully at the changes you have asked for in your Students' Charter. For each change, what responsibilities should this bring? Talk about this, and match each change with one or more responsibilities.

Back to the Normans

The Normans set up a system of control, which we now call the feudal system. It involved rights and responsibilities.

The feudal system worked like this.

- William said that all the land in England was his.

- He allowed the barons to work some of his land.

- In return for being allowed to work the land, the barons had to promise to support William and supply him with soldiers when he needed them.

- The barons allowed their knights to work some of the land they held from the king.

- In return for being allowed to work the barons' land, the knights had to promise to fight for the barons when asked.

- The peasants worked on the land in return for protection from the barons and knights.

In conclusion ...

3 Look carefully at the diagram of the feudal system above.

a) Who was the most powerful under this system? Why do you think this?

b) Who was the weakest under this system? Why do you think this?

c) Look at the barons. What do you think would happen if they decided to change things? Who would be likely to want to stop them?

In this lesson you will:

■ find out why King John and his barons quarrelled

■ work out why Magna Carta was so important then and now.

○ Key words

Freeman
A man who was free to leave his lord's lands, and who could live and work wherever he wanted to. Some peasants were freemen, others were slaves.

Great Council
A meeting of all the most powerful lords in the country to advise the king

Your turn ...

1 **a)** Draw a spider diagram to show the problems the barons had with King John.

b) Now add lines to your spider diagram to make connections between the problems.

Did you know?

The barons called the charter the 'Charter of Liberties' because it guaranteed their freedoms. It was later called Magna Carta, which is Latin for 'Great Charter'.

King John and Magna Carta

From the beginning of his reign in 1199 the barons had problems with King John. There were a lot of things they wanted to change.

> He interferes too much in the way the country is run. King Richard I was never here and we ran things in the way we wanted. King John doesn't even listen to our advice. Mind you, it's his fault when things go wrong!

> Remember his quarrel with the Pope? We didn't have any church services for five years. I was terrified we would all go to hell.

> Kings should be war leaders. King John has lost us all the lands we English held in France. He's no good!

> And what about taxation? We are taxed everywhere we turn. It's never been as bad as this. It all goes to pay for these hopeless wars in France.

> Did you hear about his nephew, Arthur? His body was found floating in the river Seine. I heard that King John ordered his murder.

What did the barons do?

By 1215, the barons had had enough. They had two options.

● Overthrow King John and replace him with someone else – but they couldn't find anyone suitable.

● Make him do what they wanted.

The barons wanted a charter, signed by King John, which would guarantee certain rights and freedoms. But they knew they would have to get him into a position where he had no choice but to sign.

The barons chose Robert Fitz Walter as their leader. Then they put together an army and sent it to occupy London. King John couldn't raise an army without the support of the barons, so he had to negotiate with them.

On 19 June 1215, after holding out for four days, King John decided to meet the barons at Runnymede, near Windsor. He signed their charter. In return, the barons agreed to be loyal.

What did the charter say?

The Magna Carta had 62 sections. **Source a** lists some of the most important ones.

Over to you ...

2   Magna Carta was not designed to help everyone in England. Copy this table. Then use **source a** plus other information on these pages to complete it.

Name of person	Did Magna Carta help them? If so, how?
Martin, a bishop	
Gurt, a peasant who worked as a swineherd	
William, a wealthy landowner	
Tom, a freeman who rented land from his lord	
Edith, who had taken over her husband's business and traded in fine cloth	
Martha, who spun wool to make cloth and who had never left her village	

a

No **freeman** can be seized or imprisoned, or stripped of his rights or possessions, or outlawed or exiled, except by the law of the land.

No freeman shall be imprisoned without a proper trial by a jury.

Justice will not be refused to anyone, nor will it be delayed or sold.

All merchants shall be free to buy and sell goods in England without extra charges [taxes].

The advice of the barons in the **Great Council** shall be sought before taxes are raised.

The English Church shall be free with her rights and liberties unchanged.

Twenty-five barons are to be elected by the other barons to keep the peace and liberties granted and confirmed to them by this charter.

■ *Some sections from the Magna Carta, signed in 1215.*

b

■ *A nineteenth-century painting of King John signing Magna Carta. Today it hangs in the House of Commons.*

What happened next?

King John didn't like Magna Carta one little bit. He got the Pope to agree that nothing and no one could limit the power of a monarch appointed by God. At that time everyone believed that monarchs were appointed by God.

Then suddenly, in 1216, King John died. His successor was his son, 9-year-old Henry. Because Henry was so young, William Marshal, the Earl of Pembroke and Henry's guardian, ruled for him. Marshal acted quickly. Together with the most powerful barons, he re-issued Magna Carta, and it was signed by themselves and Henry.

Relationships between barons and their new king seemed settled. Or were they?

In conclusion ...

3   Look carefully at **source b**.

   a) What impression has the artist tried to give of the scene at Runnymede in 1215?

   b) Use what you know about the events surrounding Magna Carta to write a few sentences saying if you think the artist got it right.

   c) Why do you think this painting hangs today in the House of Commons?

1.4c

In this lesson you will:

■ find out why trouble broke out between Henry III and his barons

■ work out whether Simon de Montfort was a hero or a villain.

Key words

Burgess

An important person in a town.

Exchequer

Part of the government responsible for collecting money.

Mark

Weight of gold or silver equal to 226.8 grams.

Parliament

A meeting of the king's advisers to grant him money, discuss problems and make laws. The name comes from the French word *parler*, which means 'to talk'.

Like father, like son?

King Henry III hated the Magna Carta he had signed when he was a child. He distrusted the barons and they distrusted him. Trouble was brewing.

> *What's all this about Sicily? He tried to buy the Crown for his son Edmund for 135,541 **marks**. And who had to raise the money for that? Us again!*

> *He's giving top jobs in the Church to foreigners. Look at Winchester. That Frenchman Peter des Roches is now bishop there.*

> *Just look at his wars! Henry's failed to get back Aquitaine and Brittany and couldn't take Poitou from the French king. And who's having to pay for all these failures? Us!*

> *Improving Westminster Abbey is all very well, but we're being taxed to pay for it.*

> *It's not just the Church. Look at the changes that Frenchman Peter de Rivaux is making at the **Exchequer**. Henry's got a lot more power now. I don't like these foreign sheriffs he's introduced. I'm losing power in my own estates.*

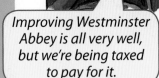

Your turn ...

1 Work with a partner to study the speech bubbles.

a) List the problems the barons had with Henry III.

b) Make a spider diagram to show how all the problems were connected.

c) Compare this with the spider diagram you made in Lesson 1.4b. Are the problems different from, or the same as, those King John's barons had with him?

> *A Council, made up mainly of nobles, was to be set up. The king could not make any decisions without the Council's agreement.*
>
> *The Council was to choose the king's chief ministers.*
>
> *A **parliament**, consisting of fifteen members of the Council and twelve other barons, had to meet at least every three years.*

■ *The Provisions of Oxford, 1258.*

Matters came to a head in 1258. The barons forced Henry to hold a Great Council (see pages 26-27) and they made some demands. These demands, shown in **source a**, are called the Provisions of Oxford.

Henry felt the Provisions of Oxford took away too much of his power. But the barons, led by Simon de Montfort, threatened war against Henry if he did not accept them. Although he signed the Provisions, Henry started to raise an army to fight the barons. In 1264 he was ready for war but was defeated at the Battle of Lewes. Henry and his son (Prince Edward) were taken prisoner.

What happened next?

Simon de Montfort was now the most powerful man in England. The other barons began to worry. Did he have too much power?

Simon was worried too. He could feel the support of his fellow barons moving away from him. He called a meeting of the Great Council. But this time, as well as asking bishops and nobles, he also invited two knights from every county and two **burgesses** from each town. This was the first time people from the towns had been invited to a Great Council. They were pleased; after all, didn't the prosperity of the country depend on them? Shouldn't they have a say in what happened?

This Council, called a parliament, began to discuss things such as taxation. This was revolutionary, and went much further than the Provisions of Oxford.

But things did not all go Simon's way. In 1265 Prince Edward escaped from prison. He called on those barons who were worried that Simon de Montfort had gone too far. Together they defeated Simon and the rebel barons at the Battle of Evesham.

Source b shows what happened to Simon de Montfort at this battle. It is rather like a cartoon strip. Start by looking at the left-hand side. First, De Montfort was killed, then his armour and clothes were stripped off. Next his head, legs and arms were cut off. Prince Edward (later King Edward I) ordered twelve soldiers to do this.

Did you know?

Henry III was released from prison after the Battle of Evesham and reigned until 1272. He never called a meeting of parliament.

■ *Illustration of the death of Simon de Montfort, drawn at the end of the 1200s.*

Hero or traitor?

2 Simon de Montfort led the barons as they tried to force King Henry III to give in to their demands. When this didn't work, he rallied them to fight against their king so they could share some of his power. Did this make him a traitor? Or did this make him a hero?

Working in a small group think of four reasons why De Montfort could be thought of as:
a) a hero
b) a traitor.

Have other groups come up with the same reasons? Reach a whole-class decision about Simon de Montfort.

The end of parliament?

Certainly not! In 1272, Prince Edward became King Edward I. When he needed money for a war, he copied Simon de Montfort's idea and called a parliament to grant him taxes. This set the pattern for all future monarchs.

From Edward's time onwards, the monarch was more and more under the control of parliament.

In conclusion ...

3 Working in pairs, draw a flow chart to show the key steps to achieving a parliament in England. Start your chart with King John and the problems his barons had with him. End it with Edward I and his Model Parliament.

Back to the start

Go back to the question with which you began this enquiry: 'Could the barons control the king?'

Work in pairs.

- One of you should write a paragraph that argues: 'Yes, the barons could control the king.'
- The other should write a paragraph that argues: 'No, the barons could not control the king.'

Share your ideas with the rest of the class and, together, reach a conclusion.

Taking it further!

1.4d

What can we learn from the stories of Robin Hood?

What do you know about Robin Hood, shown in **source a**? The story goes that Robin Hood was an outlaw who hated King John and the Sheriff of Nottingham. He lived in Sherwood Forest, robbed from the rich and gave to the poor.

No one really knows whether there was a real Robin Hood, or whether the name 'Robin Hood' was given to several different outlaw leaders. What was important was that, even in the 1300s, stories were told about outlaws and what they did. **Sources b–d** give three of those stories.

■ One of the earliest pictures of Robin Hood, drawn between 1510 and 1515.

b

But Robin pulled out a two-handed sword
That hanged down by his knee
There where the Sheriff and his men stood thickest
Towards them went he.
Twice he ran his sword right through them
In truth I to you say.
He wounded many a mother's son
And twelve he killed that day
Much did the same to the little page
For fear that he would tell.

■ One of the oldest stories about Robin Hood, written in the 1300s.

c

Robyn lived in Barnsdale with the good yeomen Little John, Will Scarlock and Much the Miller's son. Then said Little John: 'Master, tell us where we shall go, what life we shall lead. What shall we take and what shall we leave behind? Where shall we rob? Who shall we beat and tie up?'

Then said Robin: 'Look that you do no harm to any small farmer who tills with his plough. Nor shall you harm any good yeoman who walks by the greenwood thicket, or a knight or a squire for they are good fellows. However, you should beat and tie up bishops and archbishops, and don't forget the Sheriff of Nottingham.'

■ From 'The Gest of Robyn Hode', which started as a ballad sung by minstrels, and was first written down in the 1400s.

d

Then lived the famous murderer, Robin Hood, as well as Little John, together with their accomplices from among those who had lost their land and been outlawed, whom the foolish common people are so very fond of celebrating in comedy and tragedy.

■ From a chronicle by Walter Bower, written around 1440. Here he is writing about the year 1266.

What can we learn from the stories of Robin Hood?

1 What do **sources b–d** tell us about life in England around the time of King John?
2 Why do you think people sung songs and told stories about murderers, killers and thieves?

In this lesson you will:

- learn about why the English built castles in Wales

- decide which you think was the most important reason for building castles.

Why build castles in Wales?

The picture below shows Caernarfon Castle. Building began in 1283, during the reign of King Edward I of England. It cost more than £27,000, which was a huge sum of money in those days. But what were the English doing in Wales? And why did Edward want to build such an expensive building?

? *Look at the picture. Describe five ways in which Caernarfon Castle is different from the motte and bailey castle built by the Normans (page 15).*

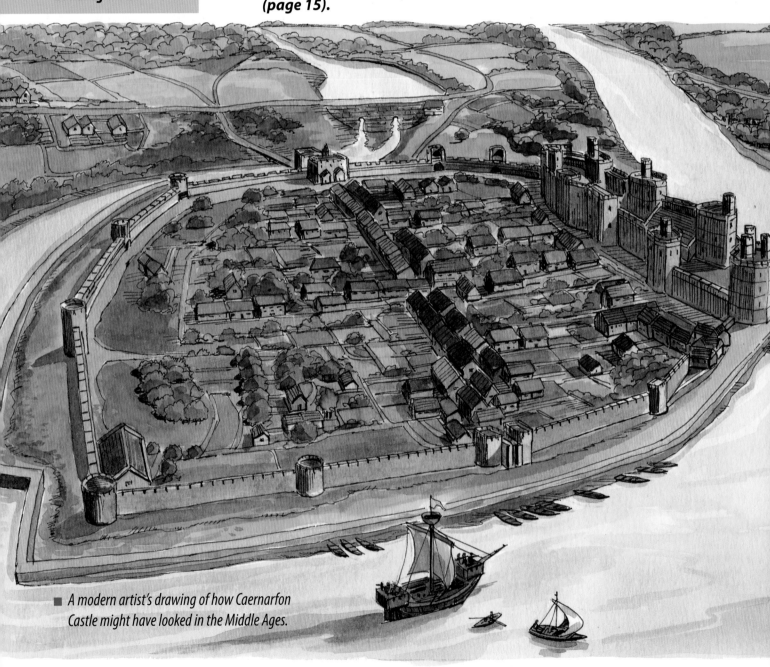

■ *A modern artist's drawing of how Caernarfon Castle might have looked in the Middle Ages.*

Shuffling the pack

1 Here are six cards with reasons why Edward would want to build such a huge castle in Wales. Read each card, then put these reasons in order: most important first, and least important last.

A Never again

In 1276, Edward I and Llywelyn the Last made a deal. Llywelyn broke this in 1282 when he attacked English castles. Edward sent an army to crush Llywelyn, and after 1284 Wales was ruled from England. Caernarfon Castle was built to make sure there would be no more challenges to English rule.

B End of Welsh rule

The last of the Welsh princes – Llywelyn the Great and Llywelyn the Last – sometimes stayed at the wooden castle at Caernarfon. Building a large stone castle would be an important sign of the end of the rule of the Welsh princes.

C Trade

Edward I's main castles were built by the sea so that the English could control trade, e.g. buying and selling food. The work on the castle at Caernarfon included building a new port.

D Protecting settlers

From the twelfth century, English families settled in Wales. The problem was that many Welsh people were not too happy to have them there. A castle could protect settlers from angry locals.

E That's cheap!

Castles were a cheap way of controlling a country. Although expensive to build, they were cheap to run. A castle only needed a small number of defenders because it was so well designed and so strong.

F Ruling

The king's officials could run a country from a castle. The officials were well protected and could make people come to the castle to pay taxes.

Vote them out!

2 You have each put your own cards in order of importance. Now you need to work in groups.

- In turn, each group member nominates their least important reason why Edward built castles.
- The card with the most votes is eliminated.

Do this until you have one card left. This will be the winner.

In the hot seat!

3 You have the chance to interview Edward I about building castles in Wales. Edward has agreed to answer up to six questions. What would you ask him? How do you think he would reply?

■ *An image of Llywelyn the Last, painted by Thomas Pryddech in the nineteenth century.*

1.5b

Were England, Scotland and Wales good neighbours in the Middle Ages?

In this lesson you will:

- find out about the relationship between England and Scotland

- recognise the significance of events for different groups of people.

England vs Scotland

England and Scotland have been playing football against each other since 1872. The first match ended in a 0–0 draw. Ever since then, the two countries have been great sporting rivals.

Look at the cartoons below.

- One tells the story of a famous victory in 1967 for the Scots against the then world champions England.

- The other tells of a victory for England against the Scots in the 1996 European Championship.

? *In pairs, tell each other the story of these two matches. Who are the heroes on each side?*

SCOTLAND TAKE TO THE PITCH TO FACE THE WORLD CHAMPIONS ENGLAND. ONE SCOTTISH PLAYER SAID THAT HE LOOKED DOWN ONTO THE LION ON HIS SHIRT 'AND THE LION ROARED'.

DENIS LAW SCORES THE FIRST GOAL FOR SCOTLAND.

SCOTLAND HAVE SCORED AGAIN!

SCOTLAND HAVE WON AND HERO JIM BAXTER IS HUGGED BY FAN.

ENGLAND TAKE THE LEAD WITH A GOAL FROM ALAN SHEARER.

ENGLAND'S DAVID SEAMAN SAVES A PENALTY FROM SCOTLAND'S GARY McALLISTER.

ENGLAND'S PAUL GASCOIGNE SCORES A WONDER GOAL...

...AND CELEBRATES.

The rivalry between the two countries lies not in football but in events that took place near the end of the thirteenth and fourteenth centuries. English and Scottish leaders fought for control of Scotland. Below are profiles of the main players.

TEAM ENGLAND

Edward I, English king 1272–1307

A bit of a legend and a good soldier. Difficult to defend against and so tall that his nickname was 'Longshanks' ('long legs'). Spent his life fighting against Scotland. On his tomb was written: *Edward I – Hammer of the Scots.*

The Earl of Surrey, 1231–1304

Did not play much of a part in the ongoing rivalry with the Scots. But, when he did (in 1297), he made a series of bad errors that led to an English defeat.

Edward II, English king 1307–1327

Very different from his father. Was a poor soldier in both attack and defence.

TEAM SCOTLAND

John Balliol, Scottish king 1292–1296

Made some silly mistakes that allowed the English to take advantage. Was unlucky to come up against Edward I.

William Wallace, Scottish legend since his death in 1305

Quick, cunning and full of good ideas. Always did well against the English. Had many successes, but was eventually let down by his fellow Scots.

Robert the Bruce, Scottish king 1306–1329

Bit of a daydreamer, but came through on the big day. Led the Scots to a famous victory over the English at Bannockburn in 1314. From then on he was the king of Scotland until his death in 1329.

Did you know?

The famous story about Robert the Bruce is that he was inspired by a spider! One night he was hiding from the English in a cave. He saw a spider building its web. If it did not succeed it tried again. Bruce suddenly thought, if he could not get rid of the English he would try and try again till he succeeded.

1 Read through the following six incidents between England and Scotland.

a) Decide whether each incident resulted in an English win, a Scottish win or a draw.

b) Look back at the main players in Team England and Team Scotland. Score their performance on a scale of 1–10, with 10 being 'outstanding'. Performance can be judged on skill, cunning and bravery as well as the ability to win. Think carefully about what you are judging for each person.

Incident 1: 1286

Alexander III, King of Scotland, died leaving only a 4-year-old grand-daughter (Margaret), to succeed him. King Edward I of England arranged for Margaret to marry his 6-year-old son (Edward), so that he would have more control over Scotland. But Margaret died on her way to her wedding in England in 1290 so Edward I did not get his way and Scotland still had no ruler.

Incident 2: 1291

The leading Scottish nobles asked Edward I to choose a king for them. Edward agreed but forced the Scottish nobles to agree that he should be Lord Paramount, which meant that he in charge overall. The nobles agreed and Edward chose John Balliol to be king of Scotland.

Incident 4: 1297

William Wallace led a Scots army against 40,000 English soldiers. The English, led by the Earl of Surrey, were trying to cross the river at Stirling Bridge when they were caught by the Scots. The Scots thrashed the English, Wallace took over running Scotland and his army invaded England (getting as far as Newcastle).

Incident 3: 1292–1296

Edward demanded that the new King John of Scotland help him fight the Scots. But the Scots thought that Edward was becoming too bossy. By 1295, they decided they would rather fight Edward than do everything he told them to. The Scots made an alliance with the French. Edward was not pleased. He sent an army to Scotland in 1296, defeated the Scots at the Battle of Dunbar and declared himself King of Scotland. Edward's victory seemed to be complete.

Did you know?

After his capture, Wallace was hanged until he was losing consciousness. He was then taken down, his body was cut open and his insides were thrown into a fire. Finally, he was chopped up into quarters and his head stuck on a spike on London Bridge. Not a nice way to go.

Incident 5: 1298–1305

Edward I was not happy and quickly invaded Scotland. In 1298 Wallace's army was defeated at Falkirk. Wallace was eventually captured and executed by Edward I in 1305 after being betrayed by fellow Scots.

Incident 6: 1313–1314

After Wallace's death Robert the Bruce declared himself king of Scotland. He attacked the English across Scotland until by 1313 the only castle left in English hands was Stirling Castle. The English king, Edward II, decided to do something about this. In 1314 he sent an army north. It was massacred by the Scots at the battle of Bannockburn. The Scots had regained their independence and the English were thrown out of Scotland.

Some of the incidents opposite had a greater impact on relations between Scotland and England than others – just as some football matches are more important than others. The more significant incidents were those that had a longer lasting impact.

Did you know?

All Scottish kings were crowned sitting on a big stone called the Stone of Scone. When Edward defeated the Scots at Dunbar, he stole the stone and took it back to London.

Over to you ...

2 a) Choose what you think was the most significant incident for both sides and explain why you think it was so important.

   b) Now choose the least significant incident for both sides and explain why you think it is the least important.

   c) Compare your choices with your partner. Have you suggested the same incidents? If so, why? Are your reasons the same? If not, how are your choices different?

In conclusion ...

3 Each incident on page 36 represents a turning point in the struggle between England and Scotland. It is your job to report on who won the war of 1290–1314. Write a report for a national newspaper. In your report you should:

   a) explain the significance of each of the events

   b) include profiles of the players.

Back to the start

Now that you have reached the end of this enquiry you might consider the following.

● How well did the English do in their attempts to win control over the Welsh and the Scots?

● Describe how you came to your conclusions about the struggle between the English and the Scots.

Next Lesson

How successful were the English against the French?

In this lesson you will:

- learn about the war that was fought against France

- show an understanding of chronology and make judgements.

War with France

From 1337 to 1453 the English and French fought a series of wars, called the Hundred Years' War. The main reason for these wars was to decide who should rule France: the King of England or the King of France? Ever since William the Conqueror had successfully invaded England, the Kings of England had owned various parts of France. Below are four maps showing which side controlled which territory at certain points of the war.

? *What story does the map tell?*

History detective

Henry this and Edward that... the names and dates can be quite confusing! Create a timeline of the kings and queens of England from 1066 to 1601. For each king or queen include their name and the dates they ruled.

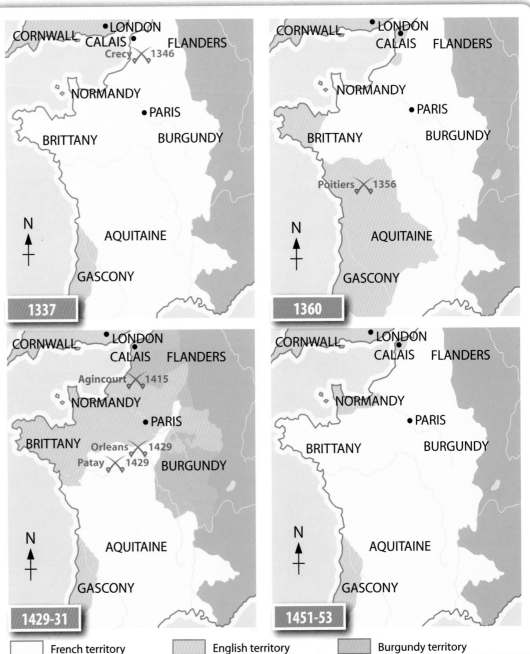

1337

1360

1429-31

1451-53

☐ French territory   ▨ English territory   ▨ Burgundy territory

Put them in order...

1 During the Hundred Years' War the English experienced both high *and* low points.

a) Read the eight most important events of the war (below).

b) Using a graph like the one shown, place these events in date order along the horizontal axis.

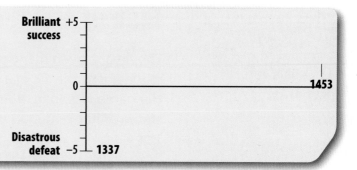

Brilliant success +5

Disastrous defeat −5

0

1337

1453

1380: English on the back foot
The English were pushed back by the French general Bertrand du Guesclin.

1346: Battle of Crecy
English longbows used to destroy the French cavalry. The English capture Calais the following year.

1415: Battle of Agincourt
War breaks out again. The English led by King Henry V are victorious. Normandy is recaptured and the battle begins a period in which much of France is conquered by the English.

1360: Treaty of Bretigny
The treaty gives England areas of France including Aquitaine and Calais, but Edward III has to give up his claim to be King of France.

1453: End of the war
Since 1429 the French kings have re-conquered nearly all of France. By 1453 only Calais is in English hands.

1337: War breaks out
French ships attack English ports, Edward III of England's army land in France but neither side gains an advantage.

1429: Turning tide
Joan of Arc leads a French army to victory at Orleans and an English army is defeated at Patay, turning the tide of the war.

1356: Battle of Poitiers
Edward III's son, the Black Prince, is victorious and even captures King John of France.

Ups and downs

2 Plot the events on this page on the graph you began above.
This is how you should score:

3 to 5: a brilliant success for the English

1 to 2: a good result for the English

0: neither side wins

−1 to −2: a defeat for the English

−3 to −5: a disastrous defeat for the English

In conclusion ...

3 Who won the Hundred Years' War? Using the information on these pages and your graph, write a paragraph to answer this question. Remember: back up your conclusions up with evidence from these pages.

In this lesson you will:

■ find out about Joan of Arc

■ use extracts of information as part of an enquiry.

Joan of Arc

There have been many pictures, statues, films and even computer games made about the life of a French girl who lived in the fifteenth century. Her name was Joan of Arc. **Source a** is a drawing of Joan and **source b** is a statue of her.

? *What clues do they give about the kind of person Joan might have been?*

■ *Joan of Arc drawn in 1450.*

■ *Statue of Joan of Arc, made in the twentieth century.*

Joan of Arc: saint or witch?

In 1429 a 17-year-old peasant girl, Joan of Arc, led a French army to victory against the English. She was captured and put on trial by the English in 1431, accused of being a witch. She was found guilty and burnt at the stake. In France, Joan became a heroine as she still is today. In 1920 she was made a saint.

Looking at the evidence

1 Use **sources c–f** to investigate the mystery of Joan. Was she a saint as the French claim, or a witch as the English claimed? Or was she neither?

a) First of all, decide if you can trust these sources. Ask yourself the following questions about each one.

What does the source say?
Do you think the source is telling the truth? Is it exaggerating?

Who wrote it?
Does the source come from the French or the English? Was the author there at the time?

Why was it written?
What are the reasons why the author wrote or said what they did?

b) Are there any other questions that would help you decide if a source is trustworthy?

Did you know?

In the Middle Ages, some women were accused of being witches. It was thought that these women were capable of sorcery or magic. This sounds a bit like a *Harry Potter* novel!

c *As a child Joan was brought up in the Christian faith, and all the local people loved her. She spent time in the fields, ploughing and guarding the animals, and she also did women's work like spinning. When she heard the bell toll for church while she was out in the fields, she came away to the church.*

■ *By a French friend of Joan of Arc, speaking at her trial in 1431.*

d *When I was 13 years old I heard a voice from God to help me govern my life. It came about noon, in the summer time, in the garden of my father's house. The first time I heard the voice I was very frightened. This voice told me often that I must come to save France.*

■ *Joan speaking at her trial in 1431.*

e *From her youth she has made and provided many spells. She has called upon devils and evil spirits, has spoken to them and has entered into agreements with them.*

Joan claims that God, His angels and His saints ordered her to do things that are forbidden by God's law. She dressed in men's clothing, short and indecent, and also in gowns and cloaks with slits up either side.

While serving King Charles, she did everything she could to persuade him not to make peace with his enemies, encouraging him to kill and shed blood.

■ *The charges brought against Joan by the English, from the trial records of 1431.*

f *Joan was a disciple of the Devil who used spells and **sorcery** to win battles. She gave courage to your enemies, and assembled them in great numbers.*

■ *From a letter written by the English Duke of Bedford to the English government in 1433.*

Decision time

2 a) Decide which of the sources, **c–f**, you trust most. Once you have thought about each source give it a mark.

5: I trust this source completely.

4: I trust this source a lot.

3: I do trust this source.

2: I am not sure if I trust this source.

1: I do not trust this source.

b) Now you need to make a decision: do you think Joan was a saint, a witch or was she neither? Base your decision on the source(s) you trust most.

Your source

3 You have used a range of sources in this lesson, some of which you trust and others you might not. Now it's your chance to produce a secondary source about Joan that you think someone could use to find out more about her life. The source that you produce could be visual or written.

Key words

Sorcery
A type of magic in which spirits, especially evil ones, are used to make things happen.

Back to the start

● Think back to the start of this enquiry: how successful do you think the English were against the French during the Middle Ages?

● What have you learned about how to review evidence to find out whether or not it can be trusted?

Next lesson

1.7a

In this lesson you will:

In this lesson you will:

- learn about the causes of the Peasants Revolt in 1381

- work together to explain the reasons why different people revolted.

The Peasants' Revolt 1381: why?

The year is 1381 and Richard II is King of England. But these are not ordinary times! Examine the paintings in **sources a** and **b** (note that **b** shows two events).

? *Describe what you can see in as much detail as possible. Explain what is happening.*

■ *A scene from the Tower of London on 14 June 1381, taken from the Chroniques de France et d'Angleterre.*

■ *Another scene from the same book, showing Smithfield on 15 June 1381*

Power in the Middle Ages was held by the king, the barons and the Church. The peasants and the workers in the towns could not vote and had few rights. But when they were hungry, felt over-taxed or that their rulers needed to be challenged, there was a course of action they could take: they could group together, refuse to do as they were told, arm themselves and take to the streets. This is called a rebellion or a revolt.

Reasons for revolt

On 30 May 1381 a tax collector called John Bampton was going about his work in Fobbing, Essex. He was collecting a tax known as the **Poll Tax**. Bampton asked the villagers for more money. But instead of paying, they told him they had already paid enough tax and would not pay any more. Bampton got angry and threatened the villagers. They chased him and the soldiers who had come with him out of the village. This was the spark for the Peasants' Revolt.

> **● Key words**
>
> **Poll Tax**
>
> A tax paid by every adult in the country in the Middle Ages. Everyone had to pay the same amount of money.

Revolution time

1 Imagine you are a group of villagers from Fobbing.

a) First, give yourselves names.
Choose a first name and a surname from the list below.

First name	Surname
Tom	Archer (someone who uses a longbow)
Rose	Blade (a maker of knives or swords)
John	Fuller (someone who shrank cloth)
Alice	Smith (someone who worked with metal)
Maud	Tucker (a clothes maker)
Robin	Walker (a cloth washer)

b) Now form a campaign group to persuade other villagers to support your cause. Use the list of reasons for revolt (below) to draw up a list of campaign slogans to convince your fellow villagers to join you in revolt.

We hate the Poll Tax which makes everyone, rich and poor, pay the same, 12p. The rich can afford to pay the tax but we cannot.

The level of our wages is set by Parliament; that can't be right and the wages are too low.

We are fed up of being owned by our feudal lords.

The French are winning the war and have started raiding villages on the coast.

Some priests such as John Ball are telling us that God made all people equal.

Our young king, Richard II, is only 14 years old. He is getting bad advice from evil men such as John of Gaunt (who is the regent), Simon Sudbury (who is Chancellor and Archbishop of Canterbury) and Sir Robert Hales (who thought up the Poll Tax in the first place). We need to rescue our king from the bad people around him.

We don't like having to give the Church two days' work for nothing every week.

This war with France is too expensive and should be stopped.

Explain your reasons

2 a) Pick a reason why the revolt broke out. Explain to the rest of your group why your reason would make the villagers so angry.

b) Now decide which reason you think is the most important. Which would make the villagers most angry?

Linking it together

3 Some of the causes of the Peasants' Revolt are linked together. See how many sentences you can write that link the causes. Here is an example to start you off …

The demand that the villagers pay a Poll Tax is linked to the king having to pay for the expensive war in France.

In this lesson you will:

- learn about what happened during the Peasants' Revolt in 1381

- discover and describe what happened as a result of decisions made by the peasants.

The Peasants' Revolt 1381: what happens next?

The year is 1381 and tempers have snapped. Peasants in Essex and Kent have refused to pay the Poll Tax and demanded change. You are about to find out what happened during the revolt by using the information and questions on this map. Use the answers on page 47 to help you move onto the next stage after you have answered each question.

London Mile End
Bishopsgate
Smithfield
Rotherhide

Stage 7 15 June Smithfield
Again you are close behind Wat Tyler as he meets again with the king. Today, Tyler demands that all land in the country is divided up and given to the peasants. The king seems to agree but suddenly the Lord Mayor of London, Sir William Walworthe, pulls out his sword and kills Tyler. For a moment it looks as if you will turn on Richard but the king calms the situation and promises you everything that you want. Should you:
a) stay in London to make sure that the king lives up to his word?
b) go home happy that the king will look after you?

Stage 6 14 June Mile End
You are just behind Wat Tyler as he meets the king. Tyler tells the king your demands including an end to feudal service, a pardon for you all and death for his evil advisers. The king agrees to the first two and hands out Charters giving you your freedom.
Should you:
a) join some of the rebels who go back into London and arrest and execute the king's leading advisers including the Archbishop of Canterbury?
b) accept the king's promises and set off home for Essex?

Did you know?

It wasn't just the English peasants who were revolting. In 1358 a group of French peasants rebelled, led by a man called Guillaume Cale. They were much nastier than Wat Tyler and his gang. When the French peasants seized one castle, they cooked a captured knight on a spit and made his wife eat some of his cooked body. Not very nice.

Stage 5 13 June 1381, Rotherhide
A few of you are lucky enough to cross the river to meet the Kent rebels' leaders at Rotherhide. Just as you arrive, a barge carrying the king and his advisers is spotted. Everyone shouts and boos the king's advisers. The barge turns round and goes back to London. Some Londoners who support us have opened the City's gates.
Should you:
a) enter the City and join in the rioting, burning the Savoy Palace and opening up the prisons?
b) return to Mile End to wait and see what the events of the next day will bring?

Stage 4 12 June 1381, Bishopsgate
After a few days marching with thousands of rebels you set up camp at Mile End, although a small group of you get as far as Bishopsgate, just outside the city walls. Should you:
a) sign a letter to the king listing your demands and asking for a meeting?
b) wait and see what happens?

Your turn ...

1 Tell your story as a cartoon strip. Each picture should have a caption.

Stage 1 30 May 1381, Fobbing

Soldiers turn up in support of the tax collector, John Bampton, who has demanded that all of the villagers pay the Poll Tax. Should you:

a) agree to pay the Poll Tax even though you have no money?

b) join with the other villagers in chasing Bampton out of the village?

Fobbing

Tell your story

2 Now tell your story in words. Few people could read in the Middle Ages so most stories were passed down through word of mouth. You might want to write a few points that remind you of what happened. Once ready, you should tell your story.

Stage 2 2 June 1381, Brentwood

You have joined up with rebels from other villages in Essex. The king has sent soldiers led by Sir Robert Belknap to frighten you into giving up your protest. Should you:

a) join with the other rebels in attacking Belknap's soldiers?

b) ignore these events and stay at home and agree to pay the Poll Tax?

Writing it all down

3 Write your story down for those in your village. Remember not many people could read and most news was passed on by word of mouth. Make your story as exciting as possible. Remember, if you reach Stage 7 you will have to write the story about yourself to be told by one of your friends. You will hopefully get the opportunity to tell your story.

Stage 3 7 June 1381, Maidstone

You hear news in the evening that a huge rebel army in Kent has chosen a man called Wat Tyler as leader of the revolt. They have also stormed Maidstone Castle and have released the popular priest John Ball. Should you:

a) become worried at what has happened in Maidstone and decide to turn back to Fobbing?

b) send a message to Wat Tyler telling him that we will see him in London in a couple of days?

Maidstone

Back to the start

Now you have found out what happened during the Peasants' Revolt in 1381 think about:

● how much power the peasants really had

● the part of this enquiry you have enjoyed the most and why

● one thing that you would like to find out more about.

Did you know?

John Ball believed it was wrong that some people in England were rich while others were poor. Ball's church sermons about this upset people in power so much that he was arrested and sent to Maidstone Prison.

N

1.7c

Taking it further!

Children making an impact in the Middle Ages

In 1381 King Richard II was only 14 years old but he clearly had a big part to play in dealing with the Peasants' Revolt. Just imagine being a king or a queen so young. You might think there must be lots of advantages, e.g. if you are in charge you can choose what you want to do every day.

However, although children could become kings or queens, they were usually told what to do by a guardian or regent until they became 16 or 18 years old. But this does not mean that some children in the Middle Ages did not make a huge impact.

Here are the factfiles of three famous children who lived in the Middle Ages. Read through each one and come to a decision about how much impact each child made. Here is how to score.

Impact rating	Description
*	Made no impact at the time and is not remembered
**	Made no impact at the time but has been remembered
***	Made some impact at the time and has been remembered by history
****	Made a big impact at the time and has been remembered
*****	Made a huge impact at the time and ever since

Factfile 1

Name: Edward V
- Became King of England in 1483 at age 12 when his father Edward IV died.
- Before his death, Edward's father arranged for the boy king to be put under the protection of his uncle, Richard of Gloucester.
- Once in control of Edward V, Richard suggested that the boy's parents had not, in fact, been married and that he should not be king.
- Edward was taken to the Tower of London with his younger brother Prince Richard. The boys were never seen again.
- The disappearance of the 'Princes in the Tower' became one of history's great mysteries.

Factfile 2

Name: Joan of Arc
- In the early fifteenth century the English and French kings were at war.
- Aged 12, Joan had dreams telling her to lead the fight to drive the English out of France.
- In 1429 she travelled to Orleans where the English army laid siege to the city. Took command of the French army which then defeated the English.
- In one battle she was hit in the arm by an arrow but calmly pulled it out before returning to the fight.
- Led the French army to Reims where the French king, Charles VII, was formally crowned King of France.
- Captured and tried, burned at the stake, in 1431.
- One of France's greatest heroines, she was made a saint in 1920.

Factfile 3

Name: Stephen of Cloyes

- On 25 April 1212, a 12-year-old shepherd boy called Stephen of Cloyes claimed that Jesus had told him to lead a crusade of the poor children of France.
- Stephen set off for Paris and was joined by up to 30,000 children. When they got to Paris the king, Philip Augustus, told the children to go home.
- Stephen did not listen to the king and led many of the children south to the port of Marseilles.
- The French children were tricked by two slave merchants who promised to take the children to the Holy Land. Instead they took them to Egypt where they were sold as slaves.

Work it out!

1 Compare your conclusions with the person sitting next to you. How many stars did your partner award and why?

2 You are to award the prize and title of 'Most important child of the Middle Ages'. Three candidates have already been nominated.

You might want to suggest an alternative candidate who you have researched on the Internet, for example Lady Jane Gray or any others that you find on www.heinemann.co.uk/hotlinks. Design the winner's certificate, which gives reasons why this person is the most important.

Answers for the Peasants' Revolt activity, pages 44–45.

Stage 1
a) You and your family are going to be pretty miserable because you have no money to pay the tax. If you don't pay you could be put in prison or even executed. You also won't be able to write a very good story so you might want to think again.
b) Dig out your old longbow and join your fellow villagers at Stage 2.

Stage 2
a) Move onto Stage 3 because Belknap's soldiers run away.
b) You have problems. You cannot afford to pay the Poll Tax and you may well be in trouble because of what happened at Fobbing.

Stage 3
a) You still have to find the money to pay the Poll Tax. You will also probably be arrested for what happened in Brentwood.
b) March on towards London. A number of peasants join you on the road to London.

Stage 4
a) Join up with the Kent rebels the next day in Stage 5.
b) Miss Stage 5 and move to Stage 6.

Stage 5
a) You get involved in a fair amount of violence, returning to your camp at Mile End in the evening.
b) Return to Mile End from where you can see the fires in the City as the Savoy Palace and Temple are burned to the ground.

Stage 6
a) You go to Stage 7 to meet the king at Smithfield.
b) You miss the events of Smithfield but you hear about Tyler's death on the way home. Because you go home early, you are not arrested as one of the leaders of the revolt but things are not good for a couple of years. The king cancels the Charters and you are forced to do feudal service. However, within months the Poll Tax is abolished and ten years later Parliament stops setting the level of wages.

Stage 7
a) You are in trouble! The king's soldiers hunt down all peasants who stayed in London and kill them.
b) You are also in trouble! You are arrested by the king's soldiers because they think that you are one of the leaders of the Revolt. They hang you by the side of the road just outside Chelmsford. You might be lucky to get back to Fobbing as described after Stage 6.

Murder! Who killed the princes in the Tower?

In this lesson you will:

■ find out why people at the time thought King Richard III had murdered the princes in the Tower

■ work with source material from the time to decide how valid the case was against King Richard III.

Case for the prosecution

King Edward IV died suddenly in April 1483. He had two sons: Edward (aged 12) and Richard (aged 9). Before the king died, he made his trusted younger brother, Richard Duke of Gloucester, Protector of the young princes. This meant that Richard would effectively run the country until his nephew, Prince Edward, was old enough to rule by himself. But it didn't quite work out like that …

In June 1483 Richard announced that his brother, the dead King Edward IV, had never been legally married to the princes' mother. This made the boys illegitimate and so neither of them could inherit the throne.

In July 1483 Richard, Duke of Gloucester, was crowned King Richard III. The two princes were never seen again. What had happened to them? Were they now dead? Had Richard ordered their murder? People have been arguing about this ever since. Remember there is no right answer. No one knows for sure whether or not Richard was involved. It's a question of weighing the evidence and coming to a judgement, based on that evidence.

The case against Richard

a

After June 1483 all the young Prince Edward's servants were kept from him. He and his brother Richard were taken to rooms further inside the Tower of London. They were seen less and less often, behind bars and windows, until finally they were seen no more. I have seen men burst into tears at the mention of Prince Edward's name for already some people suspected that he had been done away with. So far I have not discovered if he has been killed, nor how he might have died.

■ *From Domenico Mancini's* How Richard III Made Himself King, *written in 1483.*

b

For a long time the two sons of King Edward remained under guard in the Tower. Finally, in September 1483 people of the south and west began to think of freeing them by force. The Duke of Buckingham, who deserted King Richard, was declared their leader. But then a rumour was spread that the princes had died a violent death, but no one knew how.

■ *Written anonymously in* Chronicle of the Abbey of Croyland, *in 1486.*

Read and think

1 **Sources a** and **b** are the earliest written sources we have about the death of the princes.
   a) On what points do they agree?
   b) Neither of these sources say that the princes were murdered. Does this mean that they were alive when the two sources were written? Discuss this with your neighbour and write down your conclusions.

c

After his coronation in July 1483, King Richard decided that he must kill his nephews. This was because as long as they were alive, no one would believe him to be the true king. Sir James Tyrell agreed to plan the murder. He decided that the princes should be murdered in their beds. He chose Miles Forest and John Dighton to do the deed. The two men pressed feather beds and pillows hard on the children's faces until they stopped breathing. The story is well known to be true because Sir James Tyrell confessed to it when he was imprisoned in the Tower in 1502.

■ *From Sir Thomas More's* The History of King Richard III, *written in 1513.*

Act 4, Scene 3
London, the palace.

TYRREL   The tyrannous and bloody act is done.
Dighton and Forrest, who I did ask
To do this piece of ruthless butchery,
Melted with tenderness and wept at what they had to do.
Hence both are gone with conscience and remorse
They could not speak; and so I left them both
To bear these tidings to the bloody king.

■ *From William Shakespeare's play
King Richard III, written in 1591.*

But there are problems! In looking at historical evidence, just as considering evidence in a court of law, it is important to know whether the witnesses are likely to be trustworthy.

Read what is known about the authors of **sources a–d**, which you have been considering as evidence.

Tudor propaganda?

2 Take a look at **sources c** and **d**.

a) On what points do Sir Thomas More and William Shakespeare agree?

b) Do you think it likely that Shakespeare had read Sir Thomas More's book before he wrote his play?

c) Both Sir Thomas More and William Shakespeare were writing during the time of the Tudors. The Tudors were anxious to 'prove' that King Richard III was an evil king. Does this mean that we cannot trust these two sources?

Domenico Mancini
An Italian writer who visited England between 1482 and 1483. His English was very, very poor so he won't have talked to many ordinary people. He never travelled outside London, his writing is full of factual mistakes and he left England soon after Richard III's coronation.

The Croyland chronicler
Probably a monk at Croyland Abbey. Some historians think he got his information from a councillor at the royal court. Others think he got his information from John Morton the Bishop of Ely, or Margaret Beaufort, both of whom were enemies of Richard.

Sir Thomas More
He was five years old when Richard was crowned king, so his information was second-hand. He got most of his information from John Morton who was a sworn enemy of Richard III. Morton was Bishop of Ely under Richard III and later Archbishop of Canterbury.

William Shakespeare
Born in 1564, so everything he wrote about King Richard III was learned from someone else. Plays do not have to be historically accurate. However, people would not have flocked to see Shakespeare's historical plays if they had not believed them to be more or less true. Shakespeare would not have had royal support if he had written a play about an English king with which the Tudors had disagreed.

Do you have doubts?

3 **Sources a–d** provide evidence from four people who may, or may not, have had reasons to write about Richard in a bad light.

a) On a scale of 1–5, where 1 = trust totally and 5 = do not trust at all, rank the four evidence givers.

b) Now copy and complete these two statements.

i) I believe _____ can be trusted the most to write accurately about King Richard III because _____ but _____ .

ii) I believe _____ can be trusted the least to write accurately about King Richard III because _____ but _____ .

1.8b

Murder! Who killed the princes in the Tower?

In this lesson you will:

- work with source material to decide how valid the case was for King Richard III

- come to a conclusion about his guilt or innocence.

Key words

Sanctuary
A place of safety, usually a church or religious establishment.

Your turn ...

1 Read **sources b** and **c**.

a) Is there anything in these sources that would make you believe that King Richard III's court was safe for Elizabeth Woodville and her children?

b) How likely was it, then, that Richard's court would have been safe for the two princes?

Discuss these questions with a partner and reach a conclusion.

Case for the defence

In 1485 Henry Tudor, the son of Margaret Beaufort, invaded England and challenged King Richard III for the throne. In the Battle of Bosworth on 22 August 1485, Henry Tudor defeated King Richard III and became King Henry VII, and later the father of King Henry VIII and grandfather of Queen Elizabeth I.

■ *This is one of the earliest portraits of King Richard III. It was probably painted sometime before 1520 and may have been copied from an earlier, lost, portrait.*

a

b *In 1484, after strong persuasion from Richard, Queen Elizabeth Woodville [the princes' mother] sent all her daughters from **sanctuary** to Richard's court at Westminster. Christmas that year was celebrated with great splendour. There was far too much dancing and gaiety. King Richard presented Queen Anne [his wife] and Lady Elizabeth [his niece and sister of the princes] with a similar set of new and fashionable clothes.*

■ *Written anonymously in* Chronicle of the Abbey of Croyland, *in 1486.*

c *Richard decided to try all he could to make his peace with Queen Elizabeth Woodville [the princes' mother] and after a while she agreed to send her daughters to stay with Richard at Court. After this she wrote secretly to the Marquis of Dorset [her son by another marriage] advising him to forget Henry Tudor and return to England where he would be sure to be treated well by King Richard III.*

■ *Written by Polydore Vergil, historian of King Henry VII, who had defeated King Richard III in the Battle of Bosworth, August 1485.*

What about opinions after the time?

People writing later can often get a better perspective than people living at the time. This is because they have a much wider range of material to help them with their conclusions, as **sources d** and **e** show.

d *I am certain that the princes were alive when Henry came to London in August 1485. He issued a proclamation, giving out all Richard's supposed crimes and this list does not include the killing of the princes. That to my mind is proof that they were not even missing. Richard had no reason to kill them; Henry had every reason. If they lived, all he had fought for would be useless because Prince Edward had more right to be king than Henry Tudor. Henry spread the word that Richard had done the killing. Henry Tudor, murderer and liar – it is time the truth was known!*

■ *Written by historian Philip Lindsay in* Argosy *magazine, 1972.*

e *Don't you see, Richard had no need of any mystery; but Henry's whole case depended on the boys' end being mysterious. Sooner or later Richard would have had to account for the boys not being there. If Richard had killed the boys, all he had to do was to let them lie in state while the whole of London wept over two young things dead before their time, supposedly of a fever. But he didn't, and he didn't because they were still alive. But Henry had to find a way to push them out of sight. Henry had to hide the facts of when and where they died. Henry's whole case depended on no one's knowing what exactly happened to the boys.*

■ *From Josephine Tey's* The Daughter of Time, *written in 1951.*

Consider the evidence

2 Both Philip Lindsay and Josephine Tey believe that King Henry VII was responsible for the deaths of the princes. What reasons do they give?

In conclusion ...

3 Using just **source c** how likely do you think it is that Richard was innocent of murder?

Back to the start

In Lessons 1.8a and 1.8b, you 'interviewed' eight witnesses: four for the prosecution and four for the defence.
You must now reach a conclusion.

Elizabeth Woodville, the mother of the princes, wants a report from you. Write to her, explaining who you think was responsible for the death of her two sons.
Remember to back what you say with evidence.

In this lesson you will:

- find out how Henry solved some of his problems
- decide why Henry made himself head of the Church in England.

Problems and solutions

Source a shows a portrait of Henry VIII painted in 1535 when he was 44 years old and had been King of England for 26 years.

- *Portrait of Henry VIII painted by Hans Holbein in 1540.*

Look and think

1 Look at Henry VIII in **source a**.

  a) Which of the words below you would use to describe him?

proud	*scary*	*silly*	*funny*
rich	*haughty*	*strong*	*majestic*
bold	*handsome*	*smug*	*awesome* *arrogant*

  b) Choose **two** words that you think *best* describe Henry VIII. Write a sentence for each giving your reasons for choosing that word. Each sentence should begin:

  I think Henry VIII was [your chosen word] *because* …

  c) You have chosen your words because of what you believe **source a** shows about King Henry VIII. But does it show the *real* Henry or Henry as he wanted people to see him? Think about this.

  d) Hans Holbein was one of the artists employed by Henry VIII to paint royal portraits. Does this mean that we can't trust him to paint a picture showing what Henry was really like?

Problems – but did Henry always find the right solutions?

I want control.
The monasteries are loyal to the Pope in Rome and do what he says. They should listen to me and do what I say! I must be supreme ruler in my own land!

I want a son. My wife Catherine has only given me one daughter, Mary. I need a new wife. But only the Pope, the head of the Church, can give me a divorce from the old one.

I want money. I'm fighting some very expensive wars in Europe. I need to wear rich clothes and have a right royal lifestyle to show everyone what an important king I am.

How did Henry solve his problems?

Solution 1:
become supreme head of the Church of England

Thomas Cromwell, one of Henry's trusted Councillors, persuaded parliament to pass the Act of Supremacy in 1534. This ended the authority of the Pope over England's Church.

Solution 2:
get a new wife

Because Henry was head of the Church of England, he gave himself a divorce from Queen Catherine. He married Anne Boleyn in January 1533, and she was crowned queen five months later, one month after his marriage to Queen Catherine was officially ended.

Solution 3:
stop all opposition

Those people who opposed Henry taking over the Church of England were killed. These included important people like Sir Thomas More, who had once been Henry's chancellor and friend, and Bishop Fisher, a supporter of Queen Catherine, as well as many lesser known monks and priests.

Solution 4:
destroy the monasteries

Between 1536 and 1539, Henry had all the monasteries shut down. He took their gold and silver, and sold off their lands.

Compare information

2 Match Henry's solutions to his problems. Which solutions solved more than one problem? Draw a giant spider diagram, showing how Henry's problems and solutions were all linked together.

In conclusion ...

3 Go back to the beginning of the lesson and the answer you gave to question 1b. Are you surprised that Henry chose the solutions he did? You'll need to think about the words you chose when describing his character after looking at his portrait. You'll also need to think about whether the 'solutions' he chose led to even more problems.

History detective

Find out more about Henry VIII.

- Henry had an elder brother and a younger sister. What were their names?
- What was the name of Henry's nurse?
- When Henry was a child, he had a whipping boy. What for?
- What happened to Henry's elder brother?
- How old was Henry when he became King of England?
- Name one piece of music Henry composed.
- Which (and how many of each) musical instruments did Henry own?
- How many languages could Henry speak? What were they?
- What was the name of the fantastic palace Henry had built for himself in Surrey?

1.9b

In this lesson you will:

- find out the reasons Henry gave for destroying the monasteries

- work with the evidence he used to decide whether or not Henry had made up his mind before he started.

Key words

Abbot
Head monk in an abbey.

Prior
Head monk in a priory.

Destroying the monasteries

Why were monasteries so valuable? Take a look at **source a**.

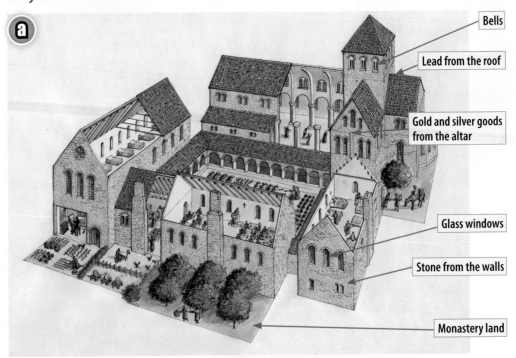

Bells

Lead from the roof

Gold and silver goods from the altar

Glass windows

Stone from the walls

Monastery land

We know that the main reason Henry VIII destroyed the monasteries was because he wanted their wealth. But even a king as powerful as Henry couldn't just take the money. He had to find reasons for destroying the monasteries in order to make his actions look reasonable and legal.

Henry's cunning plan

Henry decided to take the advice of Thomas Cromwell and send teams of inspectors out to the monasteries to find out if anything wrong was going on in them. After all, they were supposed to be holy places where monks and nuns kept their promises of poverty, chastity and obedience. The monks and nuns were supposed to look after the poor, the sick and travellers; eat simple food; behave in a Christian manner; and worship and pray several times a day. If Henry's inspectors could find any evidence of bad behaviour, this would give him a great reason to close the monasteries down.

The evidence

Sources b–g are evidence collected by Cromwell and his men. **Source h** is part of a letter written in 1535 by a monk, Richard Beereley, to Thomas Cromwell.

Your turn...

1 Look again at **source a**.

a) What does the picture tell you about why Henry VIII would want to destroy the monasteries?

b) What other reasons would Henry have had for wanting to close the monasteries? (Hint: look back at page 52.)

b **Abbot** Hexham took his share of the proceeds from piracy.

■ *From a report on Whitby Abbey.*

c *I found the **Prior** at that time in bed with a woman, both naked, about 11 o'clock in the morning.*

■ *From a report on the Crossed Friars Monastery.*

d Sister Mariana Wryte has given birth three times and Sister Johanna Sneden six times.

■ *From a report on Lampley Convent.*

e I could not find anything bad about the convent, no matter how hard I tried. I believe this was because everybody got together and agreed to keep the convent's secrets.

■ *From a report on St Edmund's Convent.*

f The Abbot of Fountains has greatly ruined his abbey, wasting his woodland and keeping six mistresses. Six days before our arrival he committed theft. At midnight he went with a local goldsmith and removed a great emerald and ruby from a gold cross. The goldsmith bought the emerald and ruby and some silver. The abbot is truly a fool and a miserable idiot.

■ *From a report on Fountains Abbey.*

g The abbot is well-beloved, having eight religious persons, being priests of right good conversation and living religiously, having such qualities of virtue as we have not found in any place.

■ *From a report about Woolsthorpe Monastery.*

h I will tell your Grace something about the monks in my monastery. The monks drink and play bowls after breakfast till ten o'clock or midday. They come to morning service drunk. They do nothing for the love of God. They have many other faults which I have no time to tell you about.

■ *From a letter by Richard Beereley (a monk) to Thomas Cromwell, written in 1535.*

Can we trust the evidence?

2 **a)** Read the two speech bubbles. Then discuss these questions.

   i) Why do you think Cromwell's men didn't always visit the places about which they were writing reports?

   ii) Which of the reports (**sources b–h**) would Cromwell have ordered to be re-written?

> The inspectors didn't always visit the religious abbeys, convents and monasteries on which they reported. Sometimes they asked people who lived nearby; sometimes they talked to monks who might have had a grudge against their monastery; sometimes they just wrote down what they thought Thomas Cromwell wanted to hear.

> Thomas Cromwell ordered the inspectors to re-write the reports that put the monasteries, convents and abbeys in a good light.

b) Write a paragraph answering the question: *Can we trust the reports Thomas Cromwell used to back his advice to Henry that the monasteries should be closed?*

Swap answers with your partner. Mark your partner's answer.

● Award one mark for each valid reason given why we can/cannot trust Cromwell's reports

● Award one mark for the examples from the evidence given to support the reasons.

What about the letter?

3 Read **source h** again. Does this make you think that the evidence collected by Thomas Cromwell might have been correct?

Did you know?

By the end of 1539, there were no working monasteries, convents or abbeys left in England. Henry VIII's income was usually around £5,000,000 a year but between 1536 and 1547 he received an extra £140,000 from the dissolution of the monasteries.

1.9c

Taking it further!

The King's Great Matter

Henry was never supposed to be king and he never thought he would be. He had an elder brother, Arthur, who married Catherine of Aragon in 1501. But five months after his marriage, Arthur was dead and no one knew (except Catherine!) whether or not they had had sexual intercourse. This was important, as you'll see later.

Catherine was a Spanish princess, and it was important that the political alliance with Spain was continued. So she was married off to Arthur's younger brother, Prince Henry. The Pope had to give special permission for Henry and Catherine to marry.

■ Portrait of Catherine of Aragon by Michael Sittoow, painted in 1502.

He agreed that Henry was right when he quoted from a book in the Bible, *Deuteronomy*, that:

When brothers live together, and one of them dies without children, then the wife of the dead brother shall not marry another, but his brother should take her and raise up children for his brother.

Everything seemed straightforward. But there was trouble ahead. Although Catherine and Henry seemed to be very much in love, they had problems producing children. A baby boy was born in 1510, but soon died. Other pregnancies followed, but ended in miscarriages. At last, in 1516, a healthy child was born, but a girl, called Mary. Henry desperately wanted a son. This was because he believed that only a son would have the strength to hold England together after his death. Girls were useful because they could be married off to secure alliances, but couldn't possibly rule a kingdom. Or so Henry thought!

Henry knew he could father a boy. His mistress, Lady Elizabeth Blount, had given birth to a healthy son. Henry had proudly acknowledged the boy as his and called the child Henry Fitzroy. The child was acknowledged by all as a prince and lived a royal lifestyle.

Henry began to believe that his marriage was doomed. This had nothing to do, you understand, with the fact that he had fallen passionately in love with the attractive, flirtatious Anne Boleyn who was sixteen years younger than Queen Catherine. Henry's lawyers began to quote from another book in the bible, *Leviticus*. This said that:

If a man take his brother's wife, it is an unclean thing. They shall be childless.

What if ... ?

1 We know what did happen, but in 1527 Henry had three choices:

   a) stay married to Catherine of Aragon and acknowledge their daughter Mary as his heir, until, which was seeming increasingly unlikely, a male child was born

   b) acknowledge Henry Fitzroy as his heir

   c) divorce Catherine of Aragon and marry again, hoping for a male heir.

   What do you think he should have done? Why?

Back to the start

Go back to the beginning of this enquiry.
How, now, will you answer the very first question:
How powerful was Henry VIII?

History detective

Find out the answers to these questions about Henry's wives.

- Which wife was six months pregnant when she was crowned?

- Which wife produced a boy child who lived to become king?

- Which wife was beheaded with a sword?

- Which wives were beheaded for adultery?

- Which wife was called the 'Mare of Flanders'?

- Which wife brought his children, Mary and Elizabeth, back to court?

- Which wife outlived Henry?

Creating an image: how was Elizabeth portrayed?

In this lesson you will:

- learn about what kind of an image of Elizabeth her advisers wanted to project

- investigate messages hidden in portraits of Elizabeth.

What were portraits for?

Have you ever seen Queen Elizabeth II? Maybe you've been part of a crowd, waving a flag and cheering when she visited your town. Maybe she has even visited your school. But even if that hasn't happened, you still know what she looks like. You have seen photographs of her in newspapers and magazines, you have seen her on TV, and you'll have seen her head on every postage stamp! But what if there were no photographs and no TV?

? *Source a is a photograph of Queen Elizabeth II dressed for a ceremonial occasion.*
What word do you think describes her best?

What did Elizabeth I look like?

Elizabeth I had portraits painted of herself, and many artists made copies of those portraits. Why? One of the ways Elizabeth could show herself to be a powerful and strong monarch was to tour the country and let people see her – to see that she wasn't the weak and silly woman many people thought a female monarch would be. But there was a limit to the number of the 'progresses' (tours) she could make. So she used portraits and copies of portraits to spread her image around the country. **Sources b–f** show a selection of portraits of Elizabeth.

Your turn ...

1 With a partner, take a look at **sources b–f**.

a) One portrait was painted when Elizabeth was 14 years old, long before anyone thought she had a chance of becoming Queen of England.
Which is it? Why do you think this?

b) One portrait was painted just after Elizabeth's death when people were looking forward to a new start with a new monarch.
Which is it? Why do you think this?

c) Which portrait do you think is the most realistic? Why?

d) Which portrait do you think is the most unrealistic? Why?

2 Go back to the portrait you thought was the most unrealistic.
Think of two reasons the artist might have had for painting Elizabeth like this.

Things are not always what they seem!

Elizabeth's portrait painters used a whole range of symbols that would have been obvious to Elizabethans but which are not too clear to us!

Pelican: Legend says that a pelican pecks its own breast to feed its young, so Elizabeth is seen as a mother who will sacrifice her life for her God and her country

Eyes and ears: Elizabeth's ability to see and hear all

Gloves: Elegance

Clothes and jewels: Power and riches

Tudor rose: Emblem of Tudor family; shows Elizabeth's regal status and her right to the throne

Fleur-de-lis: Royal emblem of France, symbolising Elizabeth's claim to the French throne

Rainbow: Peace

■ *Symbols used in portraits of Elizabeth.*

In conclusion ...

3 What symbols can you find in the portraits of Elizabeth? What do they tell us about the image she and her advisers wanted her subjects to see?

In this lesson you will:

- find out why Philip II, King of Spain, wanted to invade England and how his armada of ships was defeated

- decide how Elizabeth used this to show herself as a strong and successful queen.

● Key words

New World
The Americas, newly discovered by Spain.

Invasion danger!

Philip, the angry man of Spain

As you can see, King Philip II of Spain was not a happy man.

She is turning England into a Protestant country and the Pope in Rome has excommunicated her.

Elizabeth has refused to marry me.

She has executed Mary, the Catholic Queen of Scots.

She is helping my enemies in the Netherlands.

English ships are sinking my treasure galleons sailing from the New World.

'I'm going to teach that woman a lesson she won't forget!'

Elizabeth, defender of her country

Elizabeth was no push-over!

English merchants need to trade with the Netherlands.

I'm trying to follow a middle way between Catholics and Protestants. I hate extremists. I punish extreme Protestants as well as extreme Catholics.

Of course I had Mary Queen of Scots executed. She was plotting against me and wanted to be Queen of England herself.

I don't know anything about these Spanish treasure fleets. If Francis Drake decides to behave as if he was my little pirate, who am I to stop him?

I won't marry Philip. He will try to dominate me. He was once married to my half-sister, Mary. They both tried to turn England into a Catholic country.

'I will defend my country to my last breath!'

Read and think

1 Read Elizabeth's and Philip's thoughts. On what points do they clash? Do you think their disagreements are about religion or about power? Talk to your neighbour and share ideas.

The Armada, 1588

Philip II of Spain was the most powerful Catholic king in Europe, and he had had enough of Elizabeth and what she was up to. In July 1588 a huge fleet of 130 Spanish ships set sail for England. The plan was to:

- smash the English navy
- invade England
- get rid of Elizabeth.

But the plan went wrong. The Spanish navy sailed up the English Channel unchallenged. The Armada anchored off Gravelines, just east of Calais. Then the English commander, Lord Howard, had an idea …

He ordered fire-ships to be sailed into the middle of the Spanish fleet. The Spanish ships were forced to cut their anchor ropes and sailed, in confusion, into the open sea, where the English navy attacked them. Spanish ships were sunk, and sailors and soldiers drowned. The Spanish commander desperately tried to get his fleet home. He couldn't sail back along the English Channel and was forced to go round Scotland where the Spanish fleet was hit by terrible storms.

Only 60 ships from the 130 that set out limped back to Spain. Spain never again challenged England.

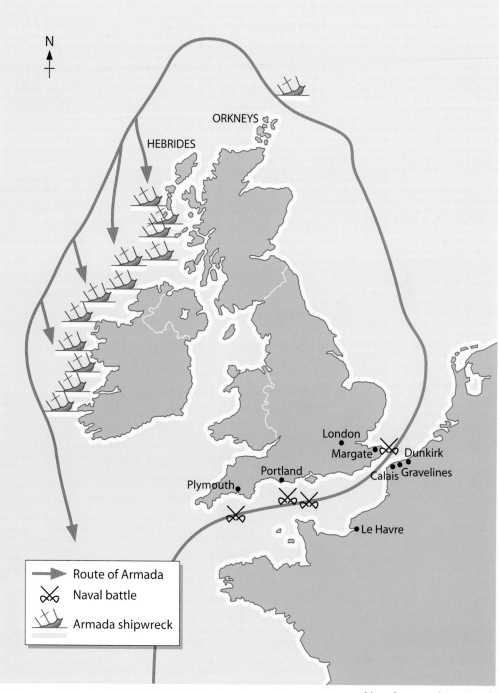

■ *Map showing the route of the Spanish Armada.*

How did Elizabeth use the Armada episode to her advantage?

Meanwhile, as the Armada was sailing up the English Channel, Elizabeth made a stirring speech to her soldiers (see **source a**). They were waiting at Tilbury, on the River Thames outside London, to repel the expected Spanish invasion. Remember that, at this time, no one knew who was going to win.

a

I am come among you, not for my own pleasure, but because I am decided, in the midst and heat of the battle, to live and die among you all. I know I have the body of a weak and feeble woman, but I have the heart and stomach of a king, and a king of England too. I think foul scorn that any king of Europe should dare to invade the borders of my realm. I will myself be your general, judge and rewarder of every one of your virtues in the battlefield. Under my general [the Earl of Leicester] I know that we shall shortly have a famous victory over those enemies of my God, of my kingdom, and of my people.

■ *Part of Elizabeth I's speech to her soldiers waiting at Tilbury for the Spanish invasion, 1588.*

Linking it together

2 Read **source a**.

a) What image of herself is Elizabeth trying to present in this speech? How is she doing it?

b) What do you think a soldier, listening to the queen speaking to him and his fellow soldiers in this way, would have made of the speech? Would he have been bored, inspired or disbelieving?

c) Imagine what he might have said about the speech when he got home, and write it down in a short paragraph.

d) Compare what you have written with others in your class. How many different attitudes have you all described?

Victory over a foreign power was always good for the image of a ruler, but Elizabeth went one stage further. She immediately commissioned a portrait of herself (**source b**); one that would link her with this victory for ever.

Did you know?

Queen Elizabeth I:
● was afraid of mice
● had a bad temper and would throw things when she got cross
● swore and spat when she lost her temper
● had black teeth because of tooth decay
● bathed just once every few weeks.

b

■ *Portrait of Elizabeth I immediately after her victory c.1588, artist unknown.*

Image-making

3 Look for images in **source b** to explain how the artist has linked Elizabeth I with the English victory over the Spanish Armada.

Back to the start

Present-day politicians have spin doctors who make sure they project the correct image to the public. How good do you think Elizabeth I's spin doctors have been? Hint: for each image you choose, ask these questions.

● What 'spin' was the artist (or author) tying to achieve?

● Do you think they were successful (a) for Elizabethans, and (b) for you? Why?

Choose at least two images.
Write a conclusion that answers the question directly.

Who was the most powerful?

In this unit you have explored the rulers and the ruled throughout the period 1066 to 1601.

Think back to your work on the eleventh century and the England of William I. By the end of William I's reign in 1087, the English monarch was in a powerful position.

Your turn...

1 In pairs, assess how much power the monarch really had. To help you make your assessment, you are going to complete a power rating grid, like the one below, using the following criteria:

- 3 points: there are no limits to the monarch's power
- 2 points: the monarch is very strong but there are some limits
- 1 point: the monarch has some control but is not too strong
- 0 points: the monarch is weak.

Each time you give a score you should explain why you have given that rating.

NB Think carefully about how you are rating each ruler – you might not be able to rate each ruler on the same factors.

Power factor	Rating	Reason for this rating
Control over the nobles		
Overseas possessions		
Power over the Church		
Ability to tax the people		
Control of Scotland and Wales		
Image		
Ability to take and give land		
Total		

2 Now move on to the end of the period and the Tudors. Complete the grid again for the last monarch or monarchs that you have studied.

3 Once you have completed your ratings, come to a conclusion by answering the following question:

Who had more power: the monarch who ruled at the start of the period 1066 – 1603, or the monarch who ruled at the end?

Make sure you back up your answer with the reasons from your power rating grid.

What was William the Conqueror really like?

What was William the Conqueror really like? Study the sources below and answer the questions that follow.

This task focuses on the skill of interpretation. Two people can have very different opinions about, or interpretations of, another person. It is the job of an historian to:

- show how opinions or interpretations differ
- explain why they differ.

William of Poitiers' viewpoint

William of Poitiers wrote *The Deeds of William, Duke of the Normans*, published in 1073, at the command of King William. This was the impression he gave of William I.

a

> *Wherever William went, everyone laid down his arms. No one tried to stop him. William was kind to everyone, especially to the common people. Often his face revealed the pity in his heart. He ordered mercy to be shown when he saw poor people, or noticed mothers and their children pleading for help. William gave many Englishmen very generous gifts. He did not unfairly take land from the English and give it to the French.*

a) What does **source a** tell you about William I?

Viewpoint from the *Anglo-Saxon Chronicle*

The Anglo-Saxon Chronicle is the story of the Anglo-Saxons. It was written by monks and scribes throughout the ninth to twelfth centuries and the Chronicles were kept in monasteries.

b

> *William and his nobles were greedy for gold and silver and did not care how they got it. The king took land from the English without pity and gave it to the highest bidder. He did not care about how the land was seized from the English or what the result was for the English people. The Normans did not care about the law, the more unlawful things were done. They raised unfair taxes and they did many other things too horrible to tell.*

b) What does **source b** tell you about William I?
c) How does the account of William in **source b** differ from **source a**?
d Why do some sources give different interpretation?
e) Give two reasons why **sources a** and **b** differ in their interpretation of William I.

How are you going to set about a task like this?

Here are some handy hints.

a) and b) These are quite straightforward questions as long as you follow this guidance. Both sources provide quite a lot of information about William I. When answering both of these questions, make sure you do the following:

- make at least three points about William
- make the points in your own words rather than just copying what the source says
- back up each point with a short quote from the source.

Here is an example from **source a**:

William really cared about the people:
'Often his face revealed the pity in his heart.'

c) This question asks you to compare the two sources and explain the differences between them. Try to make at least three points explaining how the sources differ. Think about:

- William and land
- how much William cared for the people
- William's generosity.

d) In your answer to **c)** you will have explained the differences between **source a** and **source b**. Now you need to explain in general terms why sources differ. To answer the question you need to think about the background to the source.

e) This question follows on from **d)**. In answering **d)** you should have given some general reasons why sources differ. Now use these ideas to explain two reasons why these two sources differ.

How will your work be marked? Have you:

Level 4
Identified and described different ways in which the past has been interpreted?

Level 5
Suggested some reasons for different interpretations of the past?

Level 6
Explained how and why different interpretations of the past have arisen or been constructed?

Who was the best English monarch between 1066 and 1601?

Who was the best English monarch between 1066 and 1601? You are going to award this prize to the monarch who you feel most deserves this title.

Step 1: choose your criteria

Below is a list of factors that you might use to judge the monarchs.
Choose three of these factors. For each factor, explain why you have chosen it.

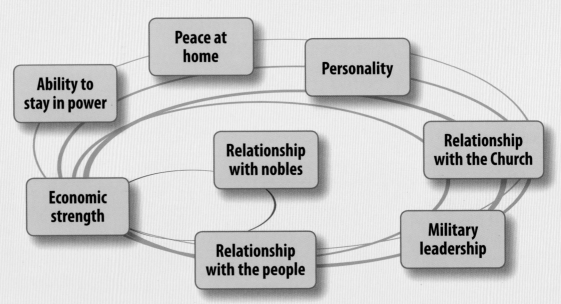

Step 2: the Final

Here is a list of some of the kings and queens who ruled England in the period 1066 to 1601. You might not have studied them all but that does not matter – just think about the ones that you have.

You need to select three monarchs to go through the final round of judging for 'Best English Monarch, 1066 to 1601'. Make your choice and for each monarch explain in one sentence why you have chosen him or her to go through.

Step 3: decision time

You now need to judge the three monarchs you have selected against your three chosen criteria. Which monarch comes out best?

Who is second? Who comes last?

For each monarch you will need to write a paragraph explaining why you have ranked them as you have.

Unit 2
Living and working

Introduction

Life for everybody in the period 1066–1601 was very different from life today. Life for most people was much harsher and people died younger. But not everything was different. As you will see in **sources a and b**, and in the following units, people did some of the same things that we do today.

Work in pairs and study these two sources closely. What you can see happening in each picture?

■ *Illustration from the Book of Hours, fourteenth century.*

■ *Painting from a sixteenth-century calendar.*

Timeline 1000 –1603

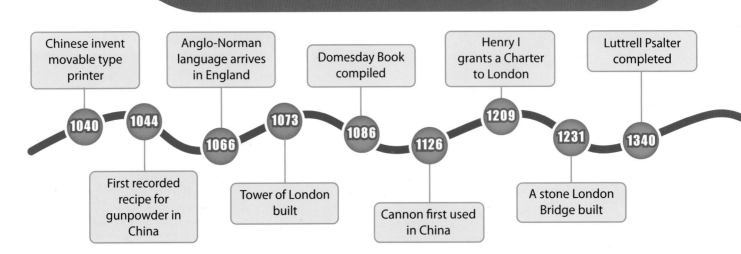

Chinese invent movable type printer — 1040

First recorded recipe for gunpowder in China — 1044

Anglo-Norman language arrives in England — 1066

Tower of London built — 1073

Domesday Book compiled — 1086

Cannon first used in China — 1126

Henry I grants a Charter to London — 1209

A stone London Bridge built — 1231

Luttrell Psalter completed — 1340

Your turn

Looking at these pictures discuss the activities that are:

- similar to activities that take place nowadays
- different from activities that take place nowadays.
- What questions would you like to ask about what life was like between 1066 and 1601?

■ *Image from a fifteenth-century manuscript.*

■ *A book illumination from the thirteenth century.*

■ *Scene from a woodcut, 1530.*

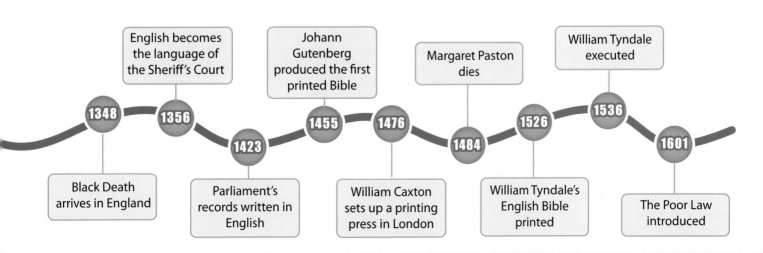

1348 Black Death arrives in England

1356 English becomes the language of the Sheriff's Court

1423 Parliament's records written in English

1455 Johann Gutenberg produced the first printed Bible

1476 William Caxton sets up a printing press in London

1484 Margaret Paston dies

1526 William Tyndale's English Bible printed

1536 William Tyndale executed

1601 The Poor Law introduced

In this lesson you will:

- find out about English houses

- understand the problems we have with the evidence.

Use your eyes!

1 Take a good look at the drawing of the village.

  a) Make a list of all the things you *know* the artist has got wrong.

  b) Make a list of all the things you *think* the artist might have got wrong.

  c) Talk to the person next to you. Are your lists the same? Where are they different – if they are – and why do you think this is?

What were English villages like in 1000?

Below is a modern artist's impression of what an English village would have looked like in the year 1000. But the person who drew this picture clearly hadn't done much research!

What's the problem?

The problem is that no houses from 1000 exist in England today. There are no drawings or paintings from those times to tell us what the houses of ordinary people looked like. So how can we find out?

We have to rely on **archaeologists** to tell us. This is because most of the houses were built from wood. The wood rotted away long ago, but archaeologists have found post-holes and staining in the ground where they think villages stood. Archaeologists can work out the size and shape of the buildings from where the post-holes are. They can analyse the staining to find out what building materials were used. From all this data, they can tell us what an English village of around 1000 would have looked like.

Archaeologists and historians have used the data to **reconstruct** a village at West Stow in Suffolk. **Source a** shows a photograph of part of the village. More than 1,000 years ago there was a real village in the same place. **Source b** is an illustration of a house of this period. The artist, who trained specially to draw reconstructions from the data provided by archaeologists, worked out that this is what these houses would have looked like.

Key words

Archaeologist

Someone who is specially trained to uncover ruins of old buildings and towns. They find everyday objects and help us to build up a picture of how people lived in the past.

Reconstruct

Build or draw something to show how it might have been, using evidence from archaeologists.

■ *Part of an English village at West Stow, Suffolk.*

■ *An artist's illustration of an English house.*

Compare the sources

2 Look at **sources a** and **b**. Which one do you think gives a better idea of what houses of around 1000 would have looked like? Why?

Think about the source

3 Look at the house in **source a**.

a) Think about what it would have been like to live in these houses. Would it have been dark or light? Cosy or smelly? Warm or cold?

b) Write a paragraph saying what it might have been like to live in these houses 1,000 years ago.

2.1b

- find out what work was done by the English who lived in villages

- construct your own English village of about 1000, using the evidence.

What about the people?

A village is a working community. Around the year 1000, a monk working in Canterbury Cathedral produced a calendar. It was written on twelve pages – one for each month. Each page showed the days of the month plus the various holy days and duties for that month. It also had a picture at the bottom of the page of the village work to be done that month. **Sources a–d** show four of those pictures.

1 Study **sources a–d**.

   a) What work are the villagers doing in each picture?

   b) For which months do you think the monk drew these pictures? How did you decide?

■ *Illustrations from the Canterbury Cathedral Calendar dated c.1000, painted by an unknown monk.*

Over to you ...

2 Now it's your turn to reconstruct a village of about 1000. Use the evidence on pages 72–77 to construct your village, complete with people, on a site like the one above. You could want to draw a sketch of what it might be like. Add notes to explain what you've done.

Make sure your reconstruction is more accurate than the one on pages 72–73!

pages 72–77

Did you know?

English villagers in 1000:
- wore simple tunics dyed in bright colours using vegetable dyes
- hadn't invented buttons
- ate plenty of vegetables
- had brains the same size as ours and were roughly the same height as we are
- lived for about 40 years
- used moss for toilet paper.

In conclusion ...

3 Take a virtual tour of the village you have created and describe your tour.

2.1c

Taking it further!

Riddles!

In the year 1000, the English were experts at jokes and riddles. Below are two of their riddles.

? *Can you work out the answers?*

> Multi-coloured, I flee the sky and the deep earth
> There is no place for me on the ground.
> But I make the world grow green with my rainy tears
>
> What am I?

(Answer: a cloud.)

> I am a strange creature.
> I grow very tall and I am hairy underneath.
> From time to time
> A beautiful girl, the brave daughter
> Of some fellow dares to hold me
> Grips my reddish skin, robs me of my head
> And puts me in the pantry. At once that girl
> With plaited hair who has confined me
> Remembers our meeting. Her eye moistens.
>
> What am I?

(Answer: an onion.)

Write a riddle

1 Write your own riddle. Then ask your someone else in your class whether they can solve it. Can you solve theirs?

2 Now write another one. Share it with others in your class. Can they guess it? Can you guess theirs?

3 Put together a class riddle book.

Next Lesson

In this lesson you will:

- discover how far life changed under the Normans

- identify key features of life under the Normans.

Changing towns

Town life: was there much of a difference?

The arrival of the Normans did not have a great impact on village life in England. However, the Normans did make a big impact on many of England's towns.

? *Look at the pictures below and opposite. Spot five differences between them.*

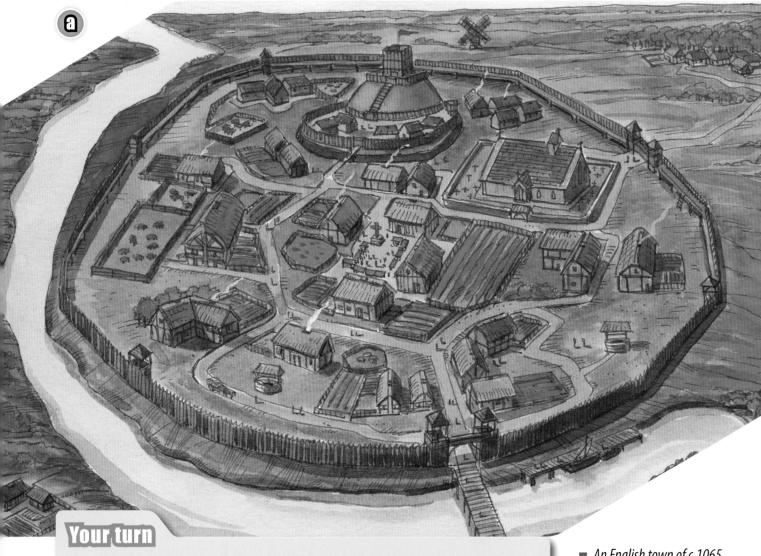

ⓐ

■ *An English town of c.1065.*

Your turn

1 **a)** Discuss the changes you have spotted with a partner or in a small group. See how many differences you can come up with between you.

   b) Despite the Normans, some features of English towns stayed the same. What similarities between the town of 1065 and the town of 1300 can you see?

Describe the differences

2 Look at the differences that you found and use them to finish the sentences below. The first one has been done for you.

- The population has grown so *there are many more houses inside and outside the town walls.*

- An increase in trade has resulted in …

- The Normans needed to control towns and the surrounding countryside so …

- The Normans believed that the church is very important so …

- The security of the town was important as was the need to control goods coming into the town. The result was …

- The Normans seized control of the forests for hunting rights. As a result …

■ *A Norman town of c.1300.*

Why the differences?

3 Use the sentences from task 2 above and your own knowledge to write a paragraph explaining how and why towns changed under the Normans. In your paragraph you could mention:

a) the changes that have taken place

b) the aspects of town life that have not changed.

2.2b

Do we speak English or French?

The English language is spoken by people all over the world. It is made up of words from a number of different languages.

- The Normans spoke a kind of French which became known as Anglo-Norman.
- Most of the people who lived in England before the Norman Conquest spoke a language heavily influenced by Saxons invaders. This was called Old English.
- Slowly, the two languages merged into what became known as Middle English.

What does it mean?

1 Here are some words from Middle English. What do they mean? Before you start, read them out loud a few times. The sound might give you a clue to the modern word.

bedde	tretee	poket	hevig
mayre	iogelour	gardin	goot
hony	souper	brigg	chirche

If you need more help working out the meanings, have a look at the clues below. Pair up the word to the clue to give you the word we use today.

- Somewhere to go and pray.
- Cross one of these to get to the other side of a river.
- An animal that produces milk to make cheese.
- An evening meal.
- Tastes sweet and is made by bees.
- An agreement, usually between countries.
- Full of flowers and other plants.
- Something to sleep on.
- You keep your money in this.
- Describes something that weighs a lot.
- Someone who is elected to run a town or city.
- An entertainer who throws things into the air.

Why did the language change?

Here are some people explaining why changes to the language took place. Their statements have been translated into modern English to make things easier for you. Read their statements carefully.

Judge, 1356
For the first time, all business in the Sheriff's Court in London is done in English rather than Anglo-Norman French. Now everyone can understand what we're doing.

Norman courtier, 1180
Most people speak English but Anglo-Norman French is still used at Court and in the law courts.

Courtier, 1300
The English kings have lost a lot of their land in France. They are starting to see themselves as more English than French.

Member of Parliament, 1360
Some Members of Parliament don't understand a word of French but thankfully everyone in Parliament now speaks in English!

Record keeper, 1423
At last, all of Parliament's records are to be written in English!

Clerk, 1410
Most people now write in a kind of English known as Chancery English. This comes from London and shows you how important the capital has become.

King Henry V, 1413
I want people to speak English at court. The French are our enemies!

Norman knight, 1086
We have wiped out the English nobility. Anglo-Norman French is now the language of England's rulers

Writer 1385
Geoffrey Chaucer's books are written in Middle English and are really popular. I think all English writers will start writing in Middle English.

Change over time

2 **a)** The reasons for change explained above and opposite are not in order. Draw up a timeline putting these changes in chronological order.

b) In your own words, describe how the spoken language changed in the period 1066–1500.
You might do this by explaining the changes to your neighbour.

Making links

3 Use the information in this unit to explain why changes to the English language took place. You might want to do this using a spider diagram. Think of at least four reasons for change, each of which you need explain in a sentence.

Did you know?

Anglo-Norman phrases are still used in Parliament, even today. When the Queen agrees to a new law; it is stamped with the words *'La Reyne le veult'*, which means 'The Queen approves'. The word 'Parliament' itself comes from the Anglo Norman word 'parler' which means 'to talk'.

Back to the start

Now go back now to the beginning of this enquiry. What have you learned about the impact of the Normans on England?

a) In groups, write down what you think was the most important consequence of Norman rule in England. Your answer does not have to come from the most recent lessons; you could also look at pages 72–79. Compare what you have written with others in your group and explain your decision to them.

b) Which aspect of the last two lessons have you found most interesting and why?

Next Lesson

In this lesson you will:

- find out about Chinese inventions

- make links between different inventions and discoveries.

Chinese inventions

? *What do you know about China?*

These days China is one of the most important countries in the world. It has a population of about 1.3 billion. That's more than 20 times the population of the United Kingdom. Many of the things that we use in our day-to-day lives are made in China.

In the thirteenth century China was an exciting place to live. The Chinese had invented or discovered a number of things that Europeans had not yet come across. **Sources a** and **b** give some examples. Describe what you can see in these pictures.

- *'Washing silk thread in the river' by Jun Wu (c.1850-1900)*

- *'The Emperor's dragon boat', drawn by an unknown Chinese artist, c. 1800-1820*

Make connections

1 Read the information opposite about some Chinese discoveries and inventions.

   a) Choose the three that you find most interesting, then summarise in your own words how the Chinese used them.

   b) Make a note of any of the inventions that we still use today.

Postal service

In the thirteenth century China had an efficient postal service. The best service was for the Emperor's letters. These were carried by trusted messengers on horseback. They were given fresh horses every few kilometres so that they could travel up to 400 kilometres a day. Second class messages were carried by foot-runners with relay-stations 5 kilometres apart.

Cannons

By the 1220s the Chinese were thought to be using cast iron bombs fired through bamboo tubes. The iron cannon was not developed until the fourteenth century, and it was not until the 1330s that the Chinese first used iron cannons. This invention was much admired by the Europeans and soon copied.

Porcelain

Discovered by the Chinese around AD 900, porcelain was in high demand by the mid-twelfth century. Europeans gave porcelain a nickname: china.

Iron and steel

Used for building large cast iron bridges and to make weapons from the sixth century onwards, 1,200 years before the Europeans.

Chinese inventions

Paper money

Trade in China was very busy. It was difficult to carry around sacks of coins to pay for goods. So, in the eleventh century, the Chinese started printing paper money.

Gunpowder

Invented in the mid-eleventh century. First used to make fireworks, then later to fire bombs and grenades through bamboo tubes.

Silk

The most important Chinese export in the Middle Ages. It was sent to the West along the Silk Road, which stretched for 6,400 kilometres all the way to Europe. Silk making had been taking place in China for around 3,000 years.

Printing

Block printing was invented in China in the seventh century. This involved carving words or pictures out of a block of wood, then covering them with ink. Around 1040 a Chinese printer invented movable type. This meant letters and characters could be moved around and reused.

Canals

The first canals were built as early as the third century. The most famous was the Grand Canal built by Emperor Yangdi in the seventh century. The Chinese also invented locks in the tenth century, meaning canals could go up and downhill.

Over to you ...

2 Many of the discoveries and innovations above have something in common. Which discoveries are linked together? Here are some clues to help you.

- This invention helps fire the weapon.
- This weapon is made out of this metal.
- This machine makes this thing that everybody wants.
- This is the best way to transport this delicate item.

a) Can you come up with any other links?

b) Explain the links between these factors in more detail. You can do this on your own or in a group by drawing a chart showing the links or by writing out your ideas for a presentation.

Why China?

3 A European visitor has arrived in China and is amazed at how advanced the country is. You are a servant of the Emperor. It is your job to explain to the visitor how and why China is so advanced. You have four headings to use.

- War
- Emperors
- Technology
- Trade

You can explain yourself in writing or in drawings using as much detail as you think your visitor will understand. Remember, you will have to explain yourself carefully.

In this lesson you will:

- learn about the Mongols and the world of Kublai Khan

- describe some features of Chinese society.

What was life like in the city of Khanbaliq?

At the beginning of the thirteenth century, when King John was arguing with the barons in England, people in Asia and even Eastern Europe faced a far more serious threat. From Mongolia came huge armies of fierce warrior horsemen: the Mongols. The Mongols destroyed villages, towns and cities killing those who got in their way. By the middle of the thirteenth century the huge Mongol Empire had spread across most of Asia.

? *Looking at the map, can you identify which of today's countries are covered by the Mongol Empire?*

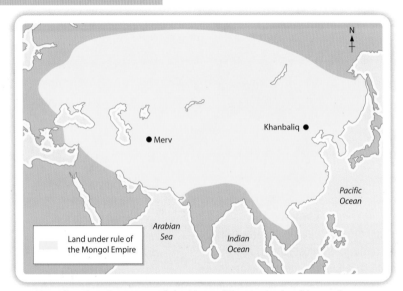

■ *Map showing the extent of the Mongol Empire in the thirteenth century.*

a

■ *Kublai Khan, leader of the Mongol Empire.*

Testing ideas

1 Divide a piece of paper into three columns, each headed with one of these ideas.

- Khanbaliq was a rich city.
- The people in Khanbaliq were clean.
- Khanbaliq was a beautiful city.

Now read through **sources b–e**. You are looking for words or phrases that support the ideas above. As you find them, write them in the appropriate column.

Did you know?

The Mongols were very fierce indeed. When they took the city of Merv (which is in Turkmenistan these days) the Mongols killed all 700,000 inhabitants and ate all the cats and dogs – or so the story goes.

Who was Kublai Khan?

Kublai Khan was the Great Khan (great leader) of the Mongol Empire from 1260 to 1294. He was the grandson of the First Great Khan, Genghis Khan. The Mongols were known as fierce soldiers but Kublai Khan was a wise and tolerant ruler. He introduced paper money and improved the water supply. Kublai Khan also built roads, canals and great cities.

The capital city of Kublai Khan's great empire was Khanbaliq, which means 'The City of the Great Khan'. Known as Beijing today, it attracted visitors from all over Asia. In 1266, three visitors from Europe arrived in Kublai Khan's capital city. One of these was Marco Polo who travelled from Venice, now in Italy, with his father and his uncle. In his book about this journey (*The Travels of Marco Polo*), the writer goes into great detail about the city.

b

There is a palace of great size and beauty with many halls and residential quarters. The roof blazes with scarlet and green and blue and yellow and every colour, so brilliantly varnished that it glitters like crystal and the sparkle of it can be seen far away.

■ *From Marco Polo's* The Travels of Marco Polo, *written c.1298–1300. This extract is about Kublai Khan's palace.*

d

They use stones that burn like logs. It is true that they have plenty of firewood, too. But the population is so enormous and there are so many bath-houses and baths constantly being heated, that it would be impossible to supply enough firewood, since there is no one who does not visit a bath-house at least three times a week to take a bath – in winter every day, if he can manage it. Every man of rank or means has his own bathroom in his house. So these stones, being very plentiful and very cheap, effect a great saving of wood.

■ *From Marco Polo's* The Travels of Marco Polo, *written c.1298–1300. This extract is about the use of coal. Although coal was used in Europe at the time, Marco Polo had not yet come across it.*

c

*The city has 12,000 stone bridges, and beneath most of these bridges a large ship might pass. There are many merchants who are very rich. Their ladies do nothing with their own hands and they live in the most elegant manner. The people are **idolaters**, subject to the Great Khan, and use paper money. They eat the flesh of dogs and other beasts, such as no Christian would touch for the world. In this city are 4,000 baths, in which the people, both men and women, keep their persons very cleanly. They are the largest and most beautiful baths in the world.*

■ *From Marco Polo's* The Travels of Marco Polo, *written c.1298–1300. This extract is about life in the city.*

e

The streets are so broad and so straight that from one gate another is visible. It contains many beautiful houses and palaces, and a very large one in the middle which has a steeple with a large bell which at night sounds three times, after which no man must leave the city. At each gate a thousand men keep guard to keep Kublai Khan safe and prevent injury by robbers.

■ *From Marco Polo's* The Travels of Marco Polo, *written c.1298–1300. This extract is about nightfall in the city.*

What is so different?

2 Write a description of what Khanbaliq was like in the Middle Ages. In your description you should quote from **sources b–e**. Use the words and phrases that you noted down in task 1 to help you. Here is an example to get you started:

Many people in Khanbaliq made a lot of money out of trade. Marco Polo wrote that 'there are many merchants who are very rich'.

Look at both sides

3 a) What is the most surprising thing you have found out about China in the thirteenth century?

b) What is the most interesting thing you have found out about China?

Back to the start

Which five words would you use to sum up life in China in the Middle Ages?

○ **Key words**

Idolater
A person who does not worship a single God. They worship an idol or idols instead.

In this lesson you will:

- find out about life on the streets in London between 1200 and 1300

- describe and explain features of London life.

Life on the London streets

London in the Middle Ages was a very different city to the London of today. People from all over the world flocked to its streets to see it for themselves. Look carefully at this map. It shows plenty of place names, which is very useful for a historian. The problem is there are a number of things a map can't tell us.

? *What three things does the map tell you about medieval London? What things doesn't it tell you? What would you like to find out more about?*

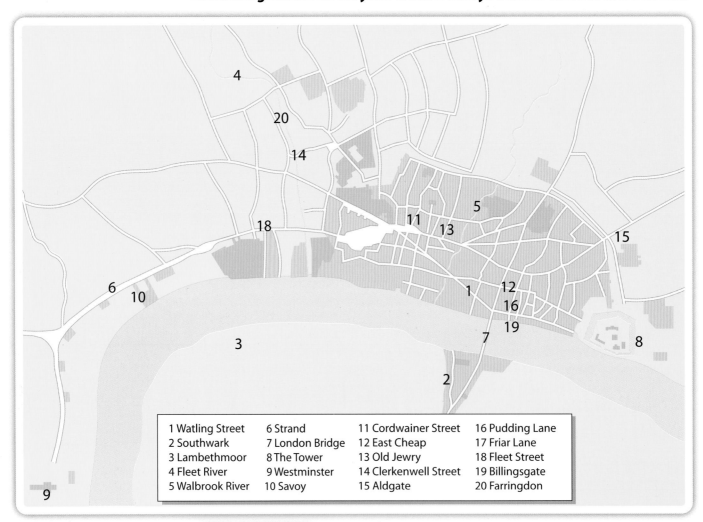

1 Watling Street	6 Strand	11 Cordwainer Street	16 Pudding Lane
2 Southwark	7 London Bridge	12 East Cheap	17 Friar Lane
3 Lambethmoor	8 The Tower	13 Old Jewry	18 Fleet Street
4 Fleet River	9 Westminster	14 Clerkenwell Street	19 Billingsgate
5 Walbrook River	10 Savoy	15 Aldgate	20 Farringdon

Your turn...

1 Imagine your family is planning to move to medieval London. You go there in advance to find out about this extraordinary city and report back. As you walk the streets you write down some notes (shown opposite). Back in your room you need to sort out these notes. Which ones will help you write about the noise of London's streets? Which ones will help you with the smells?

The streets are narrow with channels on either side. The law says that Londoners should not place any dung or filth in the streets but this is ignored. The channels are full of human waste, horse dung, kitchen waste and general rubbish.

Pigs roam the streets eating the rubbish. Sometimes they wander into people's houses.

The Thames and other rivers and streams are used as sewers. Public conveniences are built on bridges crossing the Thames, Fleet and Walbrook. The 'Long House' built over the Thames at the end of Friar Lane has two rows of 64 seats: one row for women, one for men.

In Farringdon and Aldgate there are large dung heaps.

There is a lot going on. Water bearers walk through the streets selling water. In East Cheap, butchers kill their animals and sell the meat. Shoemakers make shoes on Cordwainer Street and iron makers bash away in Old Jewry.

There are lots of beggars, all asking for money.

Balls of human waste (nicknamed puddings) are taken to Pudding Lane to be carted away by dung boats.

The streets can be dangerous when full of troublesome apprentices. Often they are drunk. They play a game of filling a barrel with large stones, then rolling it down Gracechurch Street towards the River Thames, terrorising those in its way.

It's very noisy, full of churches, convents, porters and night-watchmen all ringing their bells.

At 9pm in summer and earlier in winter, a curfew bell is sounded, after which nobody is allowed to walk the streets.

Take a look at **sources a–d**, which give extra information to help you with your report for task 1.

a

The streets are foul with human waste and the air is poisoned to the danger of men passing.

■ *King Edward III, 1349.*

b

On arriving in London we heard a great ringing of bells in almost all of the churches going on until very late in the evening.

■ *German visitor to medieval London, 1394.*

c

It smells of privies and makes for horrible sights.

■ *From a fourteenth-century report about the dung-heap in Watergate Street.*

d

The terrible smells from the public privy [toilets] next door are so strong that it has overpowered and killed a number of the monks.

■ *Monks of White Friars, 1275.*

Write your report

2 Use your notes and **sources a–d** to write your letter to your family explaining why they should or should not come to London. You need to tell them what London streets are really like, so do not hold back. Divide your report in the following way:

● a section about noises

● a section about smells

● a section about anything else you think you should mention.

You might want to use pictures to help explain, but be careful not to offend.

Compare cities

3 Look back at **sources b–e** in Lesson 2.3b. These provide a description of the Chinese city of Khanbaliq. What are the similarities and differences between your description of London and Marco Polo's description of Khanbaliq?

In this lesson you will:

- find out how people in London relaxed in the Middle Ages

- use evidence as part of an investigation.

Medieval London at play

In the Middle Ages, people had days off work and school just as they do today. Often these days off were linked to religion and were, therefore, holy days (which is how we get the word 'holidays'). On some of these days people would celebrate with a carnival.

? *Look at source a. What sports, games or other leisure activities can you see taking place?*

a

- *Painting from 1559 by Pieter Bruegel the Elder, 'The Battle Between Carnival and Lent'. The painting shows a carnival taking place in medieval Antwerp, a city very like medieval London.*

Sport and leisure

William Fitzstephen worked as a clerk for Thomas Becket (see Unit 1, Lessons 1.3a and 1.3b). It is claimed that he was present when Becket was murdered in Canterbury Cathedral. Between 1174 and 1183 he wrote a book about the life of Becket. The book begins with a few pages about life and leisure in London. **Sources b–g** are some descriptions taken from that book.

Your turn...

1 a) Read through **sources b–g**. For each one, comment on:
- the name of the sport or activity (if you don't know the name make it up)
- whether it still takes place today.

b) Design a poster for a sports festival to be held in 1180. Your festival should include as many of the activities as possible.

b When a race is about to be held between horses a warning goes up to clear other horses out of the way. Two or sometimes three boys take part as riders. Skilled in controlling horses, their biggest challenge is to prevent one of their competitors from taking the lead in the race.

c At Easter the young hold games on the river. In one game a shield is fastened to a mast fixed mid-river. A young man stands in a small boat pushed by the current and by several rowers. He has to hit the shield with a lance, splinter the lance and manage to avoid being thrown off his feet. If the lance hits the shield square on without breaking, he is thrown into the river. Hundreds of spectators crowd the bridge and galleries overlooking the river ready to laugh at those who fall in.

d In winter, the youngsters play about on the ice. Some, after building up speed with a run, slide along for a long distance. Others equip each of their feet with an animal's shin-bone attaching it to the underside of their footwear and skate along as swiftly as a bird in flight.

e Each year, on the day called Carnival, schoolboys bring fighting-cockerels to their school and the entire morning is given over to the sport, for there is a school holiday for purpose of the cockerel fights.

f After lunch on Carnival all the youth of the city go out into the fields to take part in a ball game. The students of each school have their own ball; the workers from each city craft are also carrying their balls. Older citizens, fathers, and wealthy citizens come on horseback to watch their juniors competing. They get very excited as they watch the action.

g On most festival days during winter, before lunch, hogs and boars foaming at the mouth fight for their lives; they will soon be bacon. And bulls with horns or huge bears are set to fight against hounds.

■ *Extracts from William Fitzstephen's* Life and Death of Thomas Becket, *written in 1190.*

What has changed?

2 **Sources b–g** give us a picture of leisure pursuits in the twelfth century. Imagine that William Fitzstephen, the author of those sources, has been transported through time to today. He has one month to find out about sport and leisure in our society. Your task is to interview him about the differences in sport and leisure between the twelfth century and today.

a) Draw up in groups a list of questions you would ask him.

b) Answer those questions.

Have a discussion

3 Take part in a discussion about the medieval sports and activities mentioned in **sources b–g**. There should be two parts to your discussion.

Part 1: Discuss which sports and leisure activities listed no longer take place.

Part 2: For each one, discuss why you think this is the case.

History detective

As you can see, sport (including football) was as important to people in medieval society as it is today. Choose your favourite sport and research how far back it has been played. You can use the Internet and your school library and ask your teacher for advice.

In this lesson you will:

- find out about medieval peoples' religious beliefs

- identify ways in which medieval people thought they could avoid going to hell.

Key words

Mass

The most important part of a Catholic church service, where the priest blesses bread and wine and offers them to God. Believers think that at this point the bread and wine become the body and blood of God's son, Jesus Christ.

Parish

England was divided into areas called 'parishes'. Each parish had a parish church and a priest, although sometimes parishes had to share a priest.

Purgatory

A place between heaven and hell where Catholics believe people's souls stay until their sins have gone.

Relic

Part of a saint, like a bone or lock of hair.

Hell

Many Christians in medieval England went to church and religion was an important part of their lives. But few people could read and, in any case, the services were in Latin. To help ordinary people understand Christian teaching, huge, brightly coloured pictures were painted on the walls of the churches.

■ *A medieval doom painting from the wall of the parish church in Chaldon, Surrey.*

Use your eyes!

1 Discuss the painting in **source a** with a partner. It shows the awfulness of hell and the joys of heaven.

a) Look at hell first, in the bottom half of the painting. What can you see happening?

b) Now look at heaven, in the top half. What can you see happening?

c) What is happening on the ladder between heaven and hell?

d) Why might a church want to have a painting like this on its walls?

Keeping out of hell – and going to heaven

The Church taught that:

- most people did not go straight to heaven or hell
- instead, their souls would go to a place called **purgatory**
- souls would stay in purgatory until all their sins were gone
- some souls might be there a very long time
- other souls would not make it from purgatory to heaven but would go to hell.

Medieval people believed what the Church taught and were desperate to stay out of hell, where their souls would be in torment forever – for all eternity. The Church tried to help. To get to heaven people had to be free from sin. But of course everyone had committed sins. Some were small ones, like lies, and others were huge, like murder. So what was to be done?

'I want to get to heaven!'

Matilda is a rich widow who has inherited her husband's estates and is running them well, making a good profit.

Jacob is a merchant who travels a great deal and is worried about making enough money from the wool he is selling to feed his wife and children.

Tom is a peasant who works hard, looks after his children because his wife died in childbirth, is very poor, and has never left his village.

Agnes is a woman who has worked all her life and has a little spare money.

Apart from going to **Mass** each week, the Church offered many different solutions for getting to heaven.

Solution 1: trust the priest
Priests had special powers to forgive sins. People would need to confess their sins to their parish priest. The priest would encourage people to do good deeds that could help them get to heaven, e.g. he might suggest visiting someone who was ill. But not all priests were that good!

Solution 2: use a relic
People believed that if they used a **relic** to help them pray, they would be able to get closer to God and He would be kind to them.

Solution 3: go on a pilgrimage
If the **parish** church didn't have a relic, people could make a pilgrimage to a nearby church where there was one, or to a holy place where a miracle might have taken place. The longer and more difficult the journey, the more sorry people would show they were and the less time they would spend in purgatory.

Solution 4: buy your way in
Pardoners travelled the country selling pardons. If you had a bit of spare cash, you could buy one and this would free you from your sins.

Solution 5: get help after you were dead
You could leave money to pay people to pray for your soul after you had died. If you were very rich, you could pay for a college to be set up. After your death, priests at the college would pray for your soul to speed through purgatory. They would also pray for other members of your family.

Which solution?

2 **a)** Choose one person: Matilda, Jacob, Tom or Agnes. Which solution, or combination of solutions, do you think they would have chosen? Why? Write a paragraph about it.

b) Share what you have decided, and the reasons for it, with a partner. Do you agree or disagree? If you disagree, why do you think this is?

In conclusion ...

3 Design a medieval pathway to heaven. This should show what medieval people believed they had to do to keep out of hell and get to heaven. You could decorate your pathway with drawings like the ones in **source a**.

In this lesson you will:

■ use evidence to find out what medieval people believed were the causes and cures of the Black Death

■ understand the random nature of death at this time.

Use your eyes!

1 Take a look at **source a**.

a) Write down everything you can see happening in the picture.

b) Share this with a neighbour. Have you both spotted the same things?

c) Can you make any reasonable guesses about *why* these things are happening? (Hang on to these guesses. We'll deal with them later.)

The Black Death

? *Below is a picture of flagellants. What can you see happening?*

a

■ *A picture of a procession of flagellants, from a fifteenth century chronicle.*

How did the Black Death hit?

An Arab historian, who lived through the Black Death, wrote:

A devastating plague struck East and West. Whole populations vanished. The entire world changed.

He wasn't wrong.

Impact of Black Death

The Black Death first struck in Asia in 1346.

It swept westwards, following sea and land routes used by traders and travellers.

It killed millions of animals, birds and people.

It arrived in England in the summer of 1348.

One in three people in England died of it.

Crops rotted in the fields because no one was alive to harvest them.

Animals died because no one was alive to look after them.

Churchyards were soon full. At night, cartloads of bodies were carried to the burial fields.

Whole villages were deserted because most of the inhabitants had died and those who survived had fled.

What was the Black Death?

Most historians think that the Black Death was bubonic plague. It was carried by fleas that lived on black rats, but which could be passed onto other animal and human fleas. Once an infected flea bit a person, that person would become infected. They became very tired and developed black swellings (called buboes) in their groin and armpits. Sometimes these swellings were the size of an apple. Sometimes they burst, splattering stinking pus over the person's body. The illness lasted between five and ten days. Although it was possible to recover, most people who caught the Black Death died.

Medieval doctors knew what the symptoms were and they knew they usually ended in death. But they didn't know what caused them. They knew there was a connection between dirt and disease, but they didn't know what the connection was.

So what did medieval people think caused the Black Death?

I think the answer lies in the skies. The three great planets, Saturn, Jupiter and Mars, are close together in the heavens. This has turned the air bad. We need to use natural cures to turn the air right again.

The problem is bad air. That privy stinks; the pond is stagnant and dead animals are rotting in the fields. No wonder we're dying.

This is God's doing. He is very angry with us because of the terrible sins we have committed.

I think we've got to look at the strangers in our midst. Everything was all right until they came. They could have poisoned our wells.

It's the look that does it. You've got to avoid infected people. Just one stare from someone who is sick and you're done for.

The 'cures' that medieval people used were closely connected to what they thought caused the disease in the first place.

We should do what the Flagellants do. Sing hymns and whip ourselves to show God how sorry we are for our sins.

Have you heard about the frog cure? Put a live frog on a plague sore. The frog will swell up and burst. Keep on doing this until all the plague sores have been treated. It really does work.

We must clean up the place: cart all the human waste away and stop people dumping all kinds of revolting rubbish in the streets.

Let's just get rid of people with the plague. Turn them out of the village and don't let any strangers in.

I think plague victims should be locked up in their houses and when they are dead, their clothes should be burned.

Did it work?

2 a) Using the information in this lesson, look back at the answer you gave in task 1c. Can you now work out what the people in the painting might be doing?

b) Match the 'cures' to the 'causes' of the Black Death. Take care! Some 'cures' deal with more than one cause.

c) Some of the medieval 'cures' for the plague stood a good chance of working. Which were these? Why?

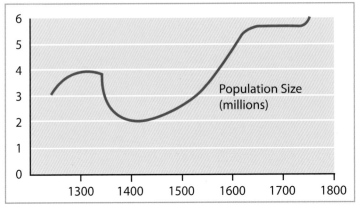

Population Size (millions)

■ *This graph shows what happened to the population of Britain because of the Black Death*

What was the impact?

3 After the Black Death, there were fewer people left to work the same amount of land. What do you think this might have meant for:

a) the lords who owned the land?

b) the peasants who worked the land?

The Black Death changed the ways in which people lived and worked. In some villages no one survived at all. In others, fewer than half the original inhabitants remained alive after the Black Death was over.

The Black Death Game

It might seem a little insensitive to play a game about the Black Death, when whether you win or lose, live or die, depends largely on luck – the throw of a dice. But think about it. That's just what it must have seemed like to medieval people. It was simply a matter of luck whether you survived the Black Death or not.

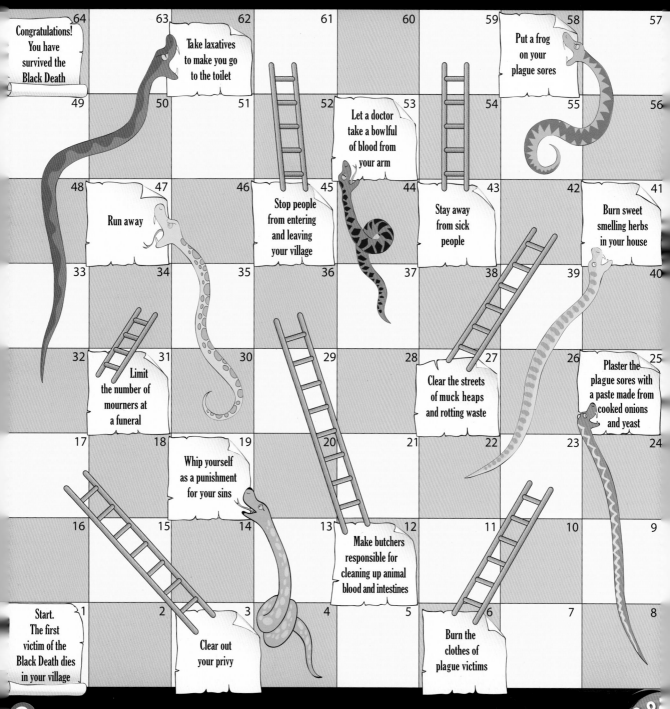

64 Congratulations! You have survived the Black Death	**63**	**62** Take laxatives to make you go to the toilet	**61**	**60**	**59**	**58** Put a frog on your plague sores	**57**
49	**50**	**51**	**52** Let a doctor take a bowlful of blood from your arm	**53**	**54**	**55**	**56**
48	**47** Run away	**46**	**45** Stop people from entering and leaving your village	**44** Stay away from sick people	**43**	**42** Burn sweet smelling herbs in your house	**41**
33	**34**	**35**	**36**	**37**	**38**	**39**	**40**
32	**31** Limit the number of mourners at a funeral	**30**	**29**	**28** Clear the streets of muck heaps and rotting waste	**27**	**26** Plaster the plague sores with a paste made from cooked onions and yeast	**25**
17	**18**	**19** Whip yourself as a punishment for your sins	**20**	**21**	**22**	**23**	**24**
16	**15**	**14**	**13** Make butchers responsible for cleaning up animal blood and intestines	**12**	**11**	**10**	**9**
1 Start. The first victim of the Black Death dies in your village	**2**	**3** Clear out your privy	**4**	**5** Burn the clothes of plague victims	**6**	**7**	**8**

? *Did you survive the Black Death? If so, how did you manage to do this?*

? *Did you fall victim to the Black Death? If so, what went wrong?*

What was life like for women in the Middle Ages?

In this lesson you will:

- find out about some of the ways women lived in medieval England

- work with source material and decide how helpful it is.

What can we learn from the Luttrell Psalter?

The Luttrell Psalter is named after Sir Geoffrey Luttrell who, around 1340, paid for his **Psalter** to be written and illustrated. It is full of pictures showing everyday life on Sir Geoffrey's estate, from the activities of his own family to the lives of the peasants. It also shows that women worked in a number of jobs.

? *Look at sources a–c, which are images from the Luttrell Psalter. Make a list of the things that the women are doing.*

Here is an example to help you:

In the Middle Ages, some women looked after animals.

- *Three images taken from the Lutrell Psalter, c.1340.*

Key words

Psalter
A book of psalms, which are holy songs and hymns from the Bible.

Your turn ...

1 Look again at **sources a–c**.

a) List three things these pictures tell us about the lives of women in the Middle Ages. Here's an example to start you off: 'Women had to go to work.'

b) Compare your list with the list made by the person sitting next to you. Have you listed the same things?

c) Put your lists together and compare your findings with the people sitting in front or behind you. Soon you will have a complete list for the whole class.

d) Are you surprised by any of the things that women did in the Middle Ages?

e) Write a short paragraph explaining what these pictures tell us about the lives of women in medieval England.

Is the Luttrell Psalter useful?

There are two ways of looking at this:

● the Luttrell Psalter is really useful to a historian trying to find out about the lives of women in medieval England

● the Luttrell Psalter might not show everything we need to know.

Did you know?

The printing press had not been invented in the Middle Ages, so every page of the Luttrell Psalter had to be written out and every picture drawn by hand.

Are pictures useful evidence?

2 Sort the statements below into two columns:

The Luttrell Psalter is useful because:	The Luttrell Psalter might not be useful because:

● it was written and drawn in the Middle Ages

● it shows the ways in which people worked on only one estate

● the artist might have made things up

● the pictures show us examples of the type of work people did

● the pictures show us some of the games people played

● the artist has painted women as well as men

● the artist is illustrating psalms, not trying to show us how people lived and worked

● it only shows us what life was like around 1330, not throughout the whole medieval period.

Take care! Some statements can appear in both columns.

How Useful is the Luttrell Psalter?

3 Use the sorting you have just done to explain:

a) how the Luttrell Psalter could be useful to a historian

b) why a historian might have to be careful using it to describe the lives of all medieval women.

Women criminals

You have already seen some examples of how rich and poor women lived their lives. Most men and women were well behaved but some were not.

? *What do you think sources a–c show?*

a

b

c

The punishments in the Middle Ages for breaking the law were very different from the punishments of today. Here are some examples.

Murder
Women who committed murder were strangled, then their bodies were burnt. But juries were often reluctant to find a woman guilty of this crime because the punishment was so awful.

Outlaws
If a woman escaped abroad she would be declared an outlaw (just like Robin Hood) and all of her goods would be seized.

Breaking feudal laws
If anyone broke a feudal law their land and all possessions would be taken away from them.

What was the Punishment?

Nagging
'Shaming' punishments were used for many women who nagged their husbands. They could be put in the stocks or the pillory, or made to wear a scold's bridle.

Witchcraft
Women accused of being witches were often tied to a ducking chair, like the one in **source c**.

Sanctuary
Sometimes people who had broken the law sought sanctuary in a church. This meant they could not be arrested. If they owned up to their crime they were allowed to leave the country. However, a judge would order that all their possessions should be seized and handed over to the king.

Be the judge

1 **Sources d–h** on page 102 are from five true court cases. You are to be the judge. In court are:
- the accused women
- those who will speak *for* them
- those who will speak *against* them
- court officials
- twelve members of the **jury** (all men).

Remember that the jury decides whether the accused is guilty or not guilty. The judge (you!) decides the punishment. Read through each case and give your judgement. If the accused are not found guilty, you must let them go free.

Key words

Jury
Group of twelve people who have to decide if someone is guilty or not guilty of the crime for which they have been accused.

Exacted
Forced to a pay a fee

Chattels
Goods and possesions

d Joan and Maud de Toffend were charged with receiving stolen goods from thieves. They come to the court and deny it. The jury say they are not guilty.

e Alice has been accused of being a witch. She is said to have cast a spell on her neighbours. She denies the charges. The jury are undecided as to whether she is guilty or not.

f Rose (widow of Robert King) and Linota (his sister) killed Robert and fled. So **exacted** and outlawed. They had no **chattels**. No one else is suspected. Linota, Robert's sister, has died.

g Joan Arsic (daughter of Robert Arsic) holds £7 worth of land in Somerton. The king is her feudal lord. Alexandra (her sister) holds £7 worth of land in the same village and the king is her lord. Both women were not married. Because the king is their feudal lord, they are supposed to ask his permission to get married. Neither did so; Joan married Stephen Simeon and Alexandra married Thomas de Haya. The jury finds them both guilty of breaking feudal laws.

h Alice of Kingham stole a tunic at Newton Purcel and fled to the church there. She admitted the theft and left the country.

■ Extracts from the records of Eyre Court (Oxfordshire), written in 1241.

Give a clear account

2 In task 1, you made a judgement about each of the Eyre Court cases. As judge, you must also make a brief speech, which includes:

- a short explanation of what each case is about
- the jury's verdict
- the punishment you decided on.

What will you say?

Think about the source

3 You have already commented on how useful (or not) the Luttrell Psalter is to a historian trying to find out about medieval women (Lesson 2.6a). How useful are these extracts from the 1241 Eyre Court? Write down two ways in which they could be useful and one reason why they might not be so useful.

Back to the start

Go back now to the beginning of this enquiry. How did you answer the very first question: 'What can we learn from the Luttrell Psalter?'

Is there anything in this enquiry that has made you change your mind? What is it? In what ways have you changed your mind?

Taking it further!

Who was Margaret Paston?

Geoffrey Luttrell's estates were not the only ones to give us evidence about the lives of medieval women. One hundred years after the Luttrell Psalter pictures were painted, a woman called Margaret Paston was busy writing letters to her husband, John. He was a lawyer working in London and left much of the running of his Norfolk estates to Margaret.

 Read sources a–c and think about these questions. What work did Margaret do on her husband's estates? What kind of a woman was Margaret?

a

April 1453

Thomas Howes has got four great beams for the private rooms and the malthouse and the brewery, three of which he has bought. As to the rest of the work, I think I must wait until you come home because I cannot get either joists or boards yet. I have measured the private room where you want your chests and accounting board, and there is no room beside the bed, even if it was moved to the door, to have space to move and sit down as well.

b

November 1453

As for cloth for my gown, I cannot get anything better than the sample I am sending you which is, I think, too poor both in cloth and in colour. Please buy me three-and-a-quarter yards of whatever you think is suitable for me. Please buy a loaf of good sugar, and half a pound of cinnamon, for there is no good cinnamon in this town.

c

April 1465

Many of the properties at Mauntby have great need to be repaired. The tenants are so poor they cannot afford to do the work. If it pleases you, I would like the peasants to have rushes with which to repair their houses. Also there is windfall wood at the manor that is of no use and might help them make repairs.

■ *Extracts from letters written by Margaret Paston to her husband John.*

Work it out!

1 What do you think of Margaret now?

2 Go back to your answers at the start of the letters. What evidence from the letters will you use to back up your opinion of Margaret?

3 Write three sentences beginning like this and with a 'because' in the middle:

I think Margaret Paston was _____ because …

4 Compare your sentences with another person. Do you agree with their answers? Can you think of reasons for any agreement or disagreement?

History detective

Find out the answers to these questions.

● Which Queen of England was nicknamed the 'she-wolf' and why?

● Who was Dame Claramunda and why was she called a 'femme sole'?

● What did Julian of Norwich do and why did people think she was important?

● There were two Queens of England called Eleanor. Who were they? Who were their husbands? Uncover two facts about each Queen Eleanor.

Next Lesson

How did the printing press change the world?

How were books produced in the Middle Ages?

? *Can you imagine living a world without computers, televisions and mobile phones? If you lived in such a world, how would you communicate with other people?*

Nowadays information can be sent around the world in an instant by email or text. In the Middle Ages, communication was very different.

? *Look at source a from the Luttrell Psalter. What can you see?*

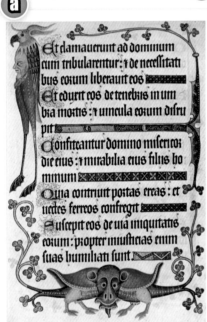 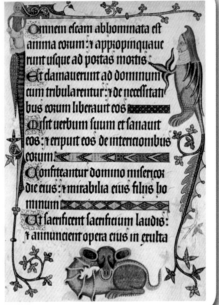

■ *Two pages from the Luttrell Psalter, c.1340.*

Writing a book

In the early Middle Ages information was sent by letter, books or in what were known as **chronicles**. The production of books and chronicles then was very different from how books are made now. They were usually written out on **parchment** by monks using quills pens. The books were often beautifully illustrated with religious pictures or showed scenes from day-to-day life. These included humans, animals or even imagined monsters. Because the books were produced by hand, they often took months or even years to complete.

Books and chronicles were expensive, so they could only be bought by the very rich. Not many children went to school and books were quite rare: in England in 1500 only 10% of men and 1% of women could read.

The impact of the printing press

? *Source b was drawn in 1498, and shows the invention that changed everything. What do you think is happening?*

Key words

Chronicle
A written record of events. It was very important in a time without newspapers.

Parchment
Thin material made from the skin of an animal, used for writing on.

Printing in Europe

In the 1440s a German goldsmith called Johannes Gutenberg started to make letters out of metal. These letters could be arranged into words and used to print pages of books. This kind of printing, called movable type printing, had been used in China in the eleventh century but now it spread quickly across Europe.

In 1455 Gutenberg produced his first printed Bibles. They were still expensive but were much cheaper than handwritten Bibles.

Printing in England

In the early 1470s an Englishman called William Caxton moved to Cologne in Germany where he learned the art of printing. He returned to London a few years later and set up a printing press in Westminster, London. Over the next fifteen years, he printed more than 100 books, including *The Canterbury Tales* by Geoffrey Chaucer (see page 139). Now books in England could be bought by people who could read but who had not been able to afford handwritten books.

What happened next

Many rulers were worried that cheaper books would mean more people could read and that they would get new ideas, which might threaten the rulers' power. Although some books were banned, they could not stop the printing press. Caxton translated books from other languages into English. Because of his printing press more and more people began to read and speak the same version of the English language.

Did you know?

The most common book that was made was the Bible. It was written in Latin because this was the language of the Church.

Your turn ...

1 Design a page of a book as if it were illustrated from a handwritten medieval book.

Choose at least five things brought about by the printing press. Write these on your page along with your reason for choosing each one. Present your page as carefully as you can. Use colours and draw scenes from life in the Middle Ages. You might like to look back through this textbook for ideas of images to include.

How did the printing press change the world?

2 Try to make connections between the changes brought about by the printing press.

a) First, think about the changes the printing press brought about. Write at least five onto a spider diagram with the word 'Changes' in the centre.

b) Now draw in links between the changes and explain each link.

In conclusion ...

3 Once you have linked the factors together, reach a conclusion about the changes brought about by the printing press.

a) Which do you think was the most important change at the time and why?

b) What was the most important change in the long term? Why?

Share your ideas with someone else in your class and listen to their point of view. See if the two of you can come to an agreement.

As a pair, share your view(s) with a group near you.

How important was William Tyndale?

Should the Bible be available in English so that more people could read it? This was one of the really big issues of the early sixteeth century.

Source a shows the death in October 1536 of a man called William Tyndale. His supposed crime was that he translated the Bible into English and, using the new printing presses, had thousands of cheap copies printed and sold in England. Describe the scene that you can see in this picture.

■ *The execution of William Tyndale, drawn by John Foxe in 1563.*

The Bible in Latin vs the Bible in English

In the Middle Ages, people were very religious. The most important book was the Bible. But the Bible was written in Latin, which most people did not understand. What's more, it was too expensive for them to buy. The Roman Catholic Church taught that it was the job of a priest to read and interpret the Bible. Every Sunday, the priest would read (in Latin) from the Bible and explain to those in church what it meant.

Before the invention of the printing press, only the very rich could afford to own a Bible. Most of them worried that if the poor did read the Bible they would start to get ideas and would try to change their world.

In the early 1500s, the idea that only a minority should be able to read the Bible was challenged by a group of people called the Lollards. Among other things the Lollards believed that everyone should be able to read the Bible in English. At that time such an idea was **heresy** and the punishment for heresy was death. Tyndale was not a Lollard, but he shared their ideas about the Bible.

> **Key words**
>
> **Heresy**
> When people have an opinion or belief that goes against the views of the Church.

> **Did you know?**
>
> People were legally killed in a number of ways in the Middle Ages: hanging, beheading, drowning. Those found guilty of heresy were often strangled, then burnt. How quickly they died depended on the how fierce the fire was.

> **Factfile**
>
> **Name** William Tyndale (c1494–1536)
>
> **What he did and what happened as a result**
>
> 1525: Completed an English translation of the New Testament of the Bible.
>
> 1526: Had English translation printed in Germany and smuggled into England.
>
> 1530: Henry VIII opposed the idea of a Bible in English and ordered his spies to find Tyndale.
>
> 1535: Was arrested by forces of the Holy Roman Emperor in Antwerp after a friend, Henry Philips, had told the authorities where he was hiding. Tyndale was put on trial for his life.

Evidence from Tyndale's trial

Look at **sources b–f**, which provide evidence both for and against William Tyndale in his trial for heresy.

If God allows me to live for a long time I will cause that a boy that driveth the plough will know more of the Bible than you do.

■ *William Tyndale speaking to a priest, 1523.*

About two years ago I bought in Colchester a New Testament in English and paid for it four shillings. I read it through many times.

■ *John Pykas, a baker from Colchester, 1528.*

Dear Reader, do not worry that it is against the law to read the word of God and do not let it stop you. If God is on our side then it does not matter what bishops or popes think.

■ *From William Tyndale's* The Obedience of a Christian Man, *written in 1528.*

Some evil people have translated the Bible into English but have twisted the words to suit their opinions. These Bibles are like poison and should be seized.

■ *Bishop Tunstall's proclamation, 1526.*

Those people who are guilty of heresy should be strangled at the stake and then burnt.

■ *Church punishment, 1535.*

Be the lawyer

1 William Tyndale has been arrested and charged with heresy, and you are a lawyer in the court case.

a) Decide whether you would like to defend (be on his side) or prosecute (be against) him.

b) Using the information in this lesson and **sources b–f**, select at least five points to support your case.

Prove the case!

2 Put together your courtroom speech either for or against Tyndale. For each point you selected in task 1, explain why it supports your case.

Remember to sum up your opinion at the end of your speech.

In conclusion ...

3 Suggest two reasons why William Tyndale should be remembered.

Did you know?

Tyndale was the first person to use a number of phrases in his translation of the Bible that are still in use today. These include:
● 'the powers that be'
● 'a law unto themselves'
● 'it came to pass'
● 'let there be light'
● 'gave up the ghost'
● 'the salt of the earth'.
He also made up words that are still in use today including 'scapegoat'.

Back to the start

Some historians argue that the printing press is the most important invention of all time. Do you agree? Explain your reasons in your answer.

Who looked after the poor in Tudor times?

Why were people poor?

? *Why are people poor today?*

How could this have happened?

1 Look at the photograph (**a**) above. Why do you think this person might be living on the streets? Think of as many reasons as you can. Sort your reasons into two groups:

- those that were the person's own fault

- those that were caused by events the person could not control.

Why were so many people poor in Tudor times?

There have always been poor people, and there probably always will be, but in Elizabethan times the numbers of people who were poor grew and grew. This was because there were a number of developments in the sixteenth century which threw working people into poverty and which made those who were already poor even poorer.

Development

A Farmers were changing from growing crops to sheep farming. They could earn more money selling wool than they could by selling corn.

B Farmers started to **enclose common land** and using it to graze sheep.

C There were a lot of poor harvests (especially 1595 to 1597) and some farmers lost all their crops.

D King Henry VIII closed all the monasteries and this meant that the poor, sick and needy had nowhere to go for help.

E More and more children were being born and the population rose.

F Food was scarce in the 1590s and prices went up and up.

G Farmers began charging higher rents.

Key words

Enclose common land
Put fences and hedges around land that previously everyone could use.

These developments hit the poor, and those close to being poor, hard.

Impact

These were some of the impacts on the poor.

1 After a bad harvest there was a shortage of food and so the price went up.

2 The increasing number of people meant there weren't enough jobs to go round.

3 People had nowhere to grow their own crops or graze their own animals. They had to buy food or starve.

4 Far fewer people were needed to look after sheep than to farm arable land. Hundreds of people found themselves out of work.

5 Landlords threw people out of their homes when they couldn't pay the rent.

6 People had no one to help them if they were sick, starving or homeless.

Match cause and effect

2 Match the developments to the impact on the poor. Take care – some of the developments had more than one impact! You might find it helpful to draw a spider diagram showing how they were all linked.

In conclusion ...

3 Use your ideas from task 2 to answer to the question: 'Why did the poor have so many problems in the sixteenth century?'

In this lesson you will:

- find out what changes the 1601 Poor Law made to the ways in which poor people, beggars and vagrants were treated

- make decisions, as an Overseer of the Poor, about what should happen to the people in your parish who asked you for help.

What was the Poor Law?

? *Who is poor today?*

No, the publisher hasn't made a mistake! This *is* the same photograph with which you began Lesson 2.8a. This time, though, we are going to ask a different question of it.

Key words

Pauper
A person who is receiving poor relief.

Poor relief
Help given to poor people by the parish so they could survive.

Vagrant
A wandering beggar.

Look and think

1 Look again at the photo (**a**) above.

a) In twos or threes, talk about what you feel when you see a person like this, begging on the streets.

b) How far do these statements match up to what you said you felt?

- *I bet they're faking it. She probably makes more money begging than she would in a regular job.*

- *I feel really sorry for him. He looks so ill. I must give him some money.*

- *Why doesn't she go to one of the refuges for the homeless? The best thing I can do is to give her the address of the nearest shelter.*

- *Someone should make him work – give him a job.*

- *What's he doing here? He shouldn't be begging on our streets.*

If your group came up with one or more of these feelings, then you would be showing exactly the same sort of mixture of emotions that the Elizabethans felt about the beggars and the poor people in their midst.

Why did the Elizabethans have to do something about their beggars?

More and more people were becoming poor in Elizabethan England. With the monasteries closed and nowhere to go for immediate help, hundreds of poor people turned to begging. Some worked alone, but many joined together in gangs, roaming the countryside, begging where they could and stealing when they couldn't. Respectable people became afraid. They were so afraid that the government decided to do something about the situation.

What did the 1601 Poor Law say?

This wasn't an entirely new law. It put together a lot of old laws and had some new ideas about the ways in which the poor should be treated.

The basic idea was that the poor should be divided into two sorts.

Deserving poor: people who were poor though no fault of their own and who, for very good reasons, *couldn't* work.

The deserving poor

- Well-off people in the parish had to pay a Poor Rate. This money was used to help the poor in the parish.
- Parishes could build poor-houses, where the poor and the sick could live and get help. Basic work was provided in the poor-house to help pay for the system. This was called 'indoor relief'.
- Parishes could provide help for people in their own homes. This was called 'outdoor relief'.
- The children of **paupers** were sent to craftsmen to learn a trade.

Idle poor: people who were fit and healthy but who chose not to work. These were people who *wouldn't* work.

The idle poor

- The idle poor were made to work.
- If they refused to work they were sent to Houses of Correction or hanged.
- **Vagrants** were whipped until bloody, then sent back to the parish where they were born.

The Poor Law said that these two classes of poor people had to be treated differently. Every parish had to appoint two Overseers of the Poor. They were responsible for making sure the Poor Law was carried out.

Being an Overseer of the Poor

2 You have been appointed Overseer of the Poor in your parish. A number of people have applied to you for **poor relief** – you can see them below and opposite. What decisions will you make? Are these people deserving or idle poor? Should they get indoor or outdoor relief, or a whipping?

Explain why you reached the decisions you did. Did the rest of your class make the same decisions?

Factfile
Alice, a widow, aged 35
She is a widow and has five children under the age of 10.

Factfile
Mary, aged 40
She been wandering from village to village, begging and stealing.

Factfile
Jack, aged 12
His parents both drowned.

Factfile
David, aged 25
He says he can't find any work at all because he is poorly.

Factfile

Thomas, aged 30,
An unemployed carpenter. He is always getting drunk and into fights.

Factfile

Peter, aged 22, who has a young wife and three children
He can't find work as an agricultural labourer.

In conclusion ...

3 Why do you think the government divided the poor into two classes and said that they should be treated differently? Was it fair to make the rich pay to support the poor?

History detective

Find out the answers to these questions.

Who or what was:

- a doxy
- a dummerer
- a clapper dudgeon
- Nicholas Jennings, the counterfeit crank
- a bawdy basket
- a beggar's cant?

How did people enjoy themselves in Tudor times?

In this lesson you will:

■ use sources to work out the differences between the ways in which rich and poor people enjoyed themselves

■ work out how far the ways in which people enjoyed themselves depended on their social class.

Rich and poor

Source a, painted by Pieter Bruegel in 1560, shows people having fun.
Source b, painted in 1592, shows a wedding party in Bermondsey, London.

Look carefully

1 **a)** Take a good look at the painting in **source a**. How many different games can you spot? Work with a partner and make a list. Which of these games are still played today? Which of the games are not played today? Can you think why?

b) Now look at **source b**. How are these people enjoying themselves? Do you think these people are rich or poor? How do you know?

a

■ *Painting from 1560 by Pieter Bruegel, 'Children's Games'.*

■ *Painting from 1592 by Joris Hoefnagel, 'A wedding at Bermondsey'.*

Become a time traveller!

2 **a)** Choose either **source a** or **b**, and jump inside the painting. What can you see? What can you hear, touch and smell? Move about among the people. Are you going to join in or just watch? Copy and complete a table like the one below.

b) Now write a paragraph, using the information in the table, that takes your class on a virtual tour of your picture.

Source	What I can see	What I can hear	What I can touch	What I can smell

Rich and poor – did they have fun in different ways?

3 Work with a partner who has chosen a different painting from yours.

Did the rich and the poor have fun in different ways? Talk about, for example, whether there is dancing, playing games or making music in both pictures. Try to decide, using the evidence from both sources, how much difference there really was between the ways in which rich and poor enjoyed themselves. Share your ideas with the rest of your class.

In this lesson you will:

- find out what theatres were like in Elizabethan times

- use evidence to work out why some people opposed the theatres.

Going to the theatre

You wouldn't think, would you, that **source a** shows something innovative and startlingly new? But it does!

So what was new here? This is a sketch of the inside of the Swan Theatre, built in London in 1595, and it shows one of the very first custom-built theatres in England. Before this, wandering groups of actors went from village to village, acting out their plays on village greens and in inn-yards. Companies of more up-market actors performed their plays in great country houses. This still went on, of course, but for the first time, in London, rich and poor could go to a permanent theatre and watch different companies of actors performing their plays. And they loved it!

Source b gives more details of Elizabethan theatres.

a

■ *A contemporary drawing of the Swan Theatre.*

b

Daily, at two in the afternoon, London has two, sometimes three, plays running. The actors play on a raised platform so that everyone has a good view. There are different galleries where the seating is more comfortable and therefore more expensive. Whoever cares to stand below only pays one English penny. But if he wishes to sit, he enters by another door and pays another penny. If he desires to sit in the most comfortable seats which are cushioned, where he not only sees everything well but can also be seen, he pays yet another. During the performance food and drink are carried around the audience.

■ *Extract from Thomas Platter's* Travels in England, *published in 1599.*

Look and read

1 **a)** Look carefully at **source a**. With a partner, work out three things you can say for certain about the Swan Theatre in Elizabethan times. Compare what you have said with the rest of your class. How many different things can your class say for certain about this theatre?

b) Now read **source b**. Which source do you think is best for helping you to understand what an Elizabethan theatre was like? Why?

c) Do you think Thomas Platter was writing about the Swan theatre? Explain your answer.

But not everyone was happy, as some of these other sources show.

c

Great disorders have been caused to this city by the gathering together of vast crowds, especially youths, to watch plays and shows. Fights and quarrels break out and all kinds of immorality.

■ *From a Declaration issued by the Common Council of London, 1574.*

e

Rich young men with nothing to do are always at the theatre. They mix with the tramps, thieves and tricksters who meet there to plot their crimes. And the plays they see are full of wickedness and cheating. Those who watch are soon persuaded to copy what they see.

■ *From a letter written by the Lord Mayor of London complaining to the Privy Council, 1597.*

d

When more than 30 people a week shall die of the plague in the City of London, then shall the plays be stopped. They may not start again until the sickness has decreased.

■ *The Elizabethan privy council issued warrants like this whenever there was an outbreak of the plague. This is an extract from one of them.*

f

Our late Queen Elizabeth of blessed memory, how well she approved of these plays, calling them 'harmless spenders of time'. Indeed, she supported the plays and players, so that they were encouraged in their actions.

■ *From Richard Brathwaite's* The English Gentleman, *written in 1641, giving the Queen's opinion.*

Read and think

2 Read **sources c–f**.

a) List the reasons why some people were opposed to the new London theatres.

b) Do you think it likely that Queen Elizabeth I would have supported theatres if they were as bad as all that?

c) Can we trust what **source f** says about Queen Elizabeth's views? The author was writing 38 years after Elizabeth's death.

Hidden messages

Plays were fun. They told stories of love and hate, adventure and mistaken identities. But sometimes they had a hidden message, too.

William Shakespeare wrote many plays. One of them was called *Richard II*, and **source g** is what one of the characters in the play says.

g

This royal throne of kings, this sceptred isle,
  This earth of majesty, this seat of Mars,
This other Eden, demi-paradise,
  This fortress built by nature for herself
Against infection and the hand of war,
  This happy breed of men, this little world,
This precious stone set in the silver sea,
  Or as a moat defensive to a house,
Against the envy of less happier lands
  This blessed plot, this earth, this realm,
this England.

What is the message?

3 Read through this speech. You could read it out loud. It's certainly very stirring! But what message is Shakespeare trying to get across to his Elizabethan audience about England? Use words and phrases from the speech to support your ideas.

Next Lesson

Life in medieval China and England

Throughout this unit you have explored how people lived in medieval and Tudor times. As you will have found out, there are many differences between life then and life today. There are also a few things that are the same.

Your turn ...

1 Make a list of some of the similarities and differences between life in medieval or Tudor times and life today.

There were also similarities and differences between cultures at the time. Below and opposite are two accounts of children living in the thirteenth century. One child lives in London, the other child lives in Khanbaliq in China.

As you read these accounts look for aspects of the children's lives that are similar and aspects of their lives that are different.

Wen Chan

My name is Wen Chan. I am aged twelve years old and I live in a large wooden house in the city of Khanbaliq. My father works as an engineer for our Emperor Kublai Khan. His job is to build canals that bring clean water into the city for people to drink. We also have clean water for public baths. I am very excited because tonight there is a festival and there will be fireworks; I really enjoy seeing the fireworks go off, they make such pretty colours. Before we go to the fireworks we will drink tea which is made when you add boiling water to the leaves from the tea plant.

I help my mother run the household. We keep chickens and pigs at the back of our house; every day I collect the eggs laid by the chickens. My father is the person in our family who keeps the money; it is made out of paper and he uses it to buy myself and my mother beautiful dresses made of silk. Last week my father was ill with a headache. He called for a doctor who came and stuck needles in him. This is known as acupuncture. It seemed to work; my father got better very quickly.

Adele Chandler

My name is Adele Chandler. I am eleven years old and I live in London. My father is an important person; he is one of the best candle makers in London. He makes his candles from beeswax and sells them to churches across London. We have to go to church every week to watch his candles burn. We live in a big wooden house in Aldgate. We want to move further to Westminster because the water does not taste good where we are living. It is soon Carnival and we will go to watch the games held on the River Thames. It makes me laugh when the boys fall into the water. When it is Carnival we are allowed to drink ale although I prefer a cup of warm milk.

We have servants who look after the animals at the back of the house; we have pigs, ducks and chickens. Every day I collect the eggs from both ducks and chickens. Next week is my birthday and I think that my father has been saving his coins to buy me the best linen underwear and a green woollen dress. I hope I will not get too hot wearing my new dress; last week I said I felt hot and my mother thought that I was ill. She said that she would send for the apothecary who would come and put a potion of ground earthworms on my head. I told my mother that I did not feel ill any more.

Over to you ...

1 What are the similarities in the lives of Wen and Adele?

2 What are the differences between the lives of Wen and Adele?

Now try this ...

3 Now, using the information that you have about life in China and England in the Middle Ages, complete *either* task a) *or* task b).

a) Imagine that Adele and Wen have heard about each other from sailors who have travelled between England and China. Write a letter that either Adele might have written to Wen or that Wen might have written to Adele. The letter should say what they find strange and interesting about each others' lives – and what they find much the same.

b) Organise a class debate on whether life for children was better in Khanbaliq or London.

Assessment 1

Was life hard for medieval peasants?

Study the sources below and answer the questions that follow.

- *This picture of peasants dancing was painted in the fifteenth century.*

1. What does this picture tell you about peasants' lives in the fifteenth century?

- *From* Pierce the Ploughman's Creed, *which was written anonymously in c.1390.*

As I went by the way, weeping for sorrow, I saw a poor man hanging on to a plough. His coat was full of coarse material; his hood was full of holes and his hair stuck out of it. As he trod the soil his toes stuck out of his worn shoes with their thick soles. His stockings hung about his legs and he was covered with mud as he followed the plough. He had two mittens, scantily made of rough stuff, with worn out fingers and thick with muck.

2. Sources a and **b** give very different impressions of the lives of peasants. Does this mean one of them must be wrong?

- *From a modern history textbook.*

Peasants could grow whatever they liked on their own plots of land around their houses. These personal plots were called tofts. On their tofts peasants grew vegetables and herbs, and kept bees and various livestock, including cattle, sheep, pigs and poultry.

3. Source c was written hundreds of years after medieval times. Does **source a** or **source b** back it up best?

- *From a history website. Find out more at www.heinemann.co.uk/ hotlinks*

The lifestyle of peasants in medieval England was extremely hard and harsh. Many worked in fields owned by the lords and their lives were controlled by the farming year. People were covered with dirt, fleas and lice.

4. Sources c and **d** were both written by modern historians. Why do they seem to disagree about what it was like to be a medieval peasant?

5. Use these four sources and your own knowledge to answer the question: *Was life for medieval peasants really hard?*

How are you going to set about a task like this?

1 a) Don't just **describe** what you can see. **Think** about what you can see. What conclusions can you draw? For example, if some of the peasants were wearing richly embroidered clothes, you could draw the conclusion (called an **inference**) that some peasants were very rich.

b) You are being asked to compare, or cross reference, two sources. On the surface, the two sources seem very different. One shows some peasants dancing. The other describes a desperately poor ploughman.

- Could the wretched ploughman be in that condition because he was ploughing through mud in the pouring rain?
- Could he have some better clothes to put on for an evening out?
- Would the occupations of the peasants make a difference?
- How important is it that we don't know who created each source?
- Might they describe conditions in different parts of the country?

c) This is a different sort of **cross-referencing** question. You need to decide which source from the time (**a** or **b**) best backs a secondary source, **source c**, which was written later. Don't just look at the surface features of the sources but look behind them and the inferences you can draw. Then reach a decision, and explain why you have reached it.

d) Ask yourself how historians reach conclusions. These two historians seem to have **interpreted** the past in different ways. How could this have happened?

e) Use your **knowledge** as well as the **sources**. Look back to Lessons 2.1a, b and c to remind yourself what life was like for medieval peasants.

- How far do the sources support what you know and how far do they say something else?
- So, was life for medieval peasants hard?
- Do the sources tell you this – or your own knowledge?

Remember, the sources might be unreliable and might only give you a snapshot of a particular place at a certain time. So while things may be bad, or good, for a person or a place, that doesn't necessarily mean they are bad or good everywhere.

How will your work be marked? Have you:

Level 4
Described the lives of some peasants, showing that you understand that there were some differences within the same period?

Shown that you understand that the past has been interpreted in different ways?

Used the right sort of information to answer the question? Written in clear sentences using the right dates and historical words?

Level 5
Shown that you understand that the lives of medieval peasants differed from time to time and place to place?

Begun to suggest why the past has been interpreted in different ways?

Selected information that best answers the question in a sensible, structured way?

Level 6
Begun to sort out why the lives of medieval peasants might have differed from time to time and place to place?

Begun to explain how and why different interpretations of the past have been made?

Selected and organised the right sort of information that best answers the question?

What were the most important Chinese discoveries or inventions, and why?

It is 1295. Marco Polo has just arrived back in Italy. He has fantastic stories to tell about life in China and about Chinese discoveries and inventions. He asks you to design a poster. The poster must tell thirteenth-century Europeans about the four most important inventions (or discoveries) he saw, and explain why they are so important.

Make your poster as eye-catching and informative as you can.

You've probably got lots of ideas already – look back to Lessons 2.3a and b to remind yourself of what these could be. Here are some of them.

How are you going to set about a task like this?

Here are some handy hints!

- Read Lessons 2.3a and b, which tell you all about the discoveries and inventions made in China.
- Choose the four that you think are the most important.
- When making your choice, think about the next part of the task. You have to explain why Marco Polo thinks they are so important. So when you are choosing the inventions and/or discoveries, try to think yourself into Marco Polo's shoes. Why would he have thought they were important?
- Work out what you are going to write about why Marco Polo would have thought them important. Make what you say sharp, snappy and to the point.

How are you going to structure your poster?

There are lots of different ways you could structure your poster. But whatever methods you use, remember to plan it first!

Planning

Make sure your poster is eye-catching.

- Are you going to have a big, bold heading that will make people stop and look?
- Are you going to put Marco Polo on it?
- Are you going to put pictures of the inventions/discoveries on to your poster?
- How are you going to arrange them?
- Where are you going to put the information?

Designing

In many ways planning and designing go hand in hand. This is because you have to think of the materials you are going to use when you are at the planning stage.

How will your work be marked?

Have you:

Level 4

Described some of the most important discoveries and/or inventions in thirteenth-century China?

Said that they were important?

Used dates and historical words correctly?

Begun to produce structured work?

Level 5

Described some of the most important discoveries and/or inventions in thirteenth-century China and putting them into the right time frame?

Selected and used information in order to explain why they were important, using proper historical terms?

Produced structured work?

Level 6

Shown that you understand that different sorts of inventions and/or discoveries existed within China at the same time?

Shown what rules you have used to judge which were the most important?

Selected, organised and used relevant information, using the right historical words, to produce structured work?

Introduction

Unit 3 — Moving and travelling

Medieval people are on the move! They're going to markets and to towns; they're going on pilgrimages and crusades; they're moving to different countries; they're trading with different races of people and they're exploring the world.

? *Medieval people may have been on the move, but how were they going to get to wherever they were going? Match the people to their most likely method of transport.*

Timeline 1000–1603

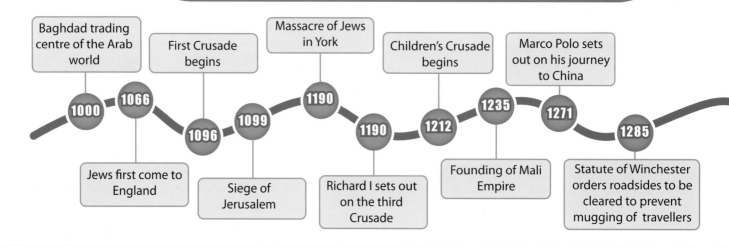

Baghdad trading centre of the Arab world — 1000

First Crusade begins — 1066

1066 — Jews first come to England

1096 — Siege of Jerusalem

1099

Massacre of Jews in York — 1190

1190 — Richard I sets out on the third Crusade

Children's Crusade begins — 1212

1235 — Founding of Mali Empire

Marco Polo sets out on his journey to China — 1271

1285 — Statute of Winchester orders roadsides to be cleared to prevent mugging of travellers

? *There's one method of transport that was used by most people in the medieval world and it isn't shown here. What is it?*

? *You've matched the people to the transport, but what now?*
What questions do you want to ask about medieval people on the move?

This unit should answer all your questions. Read on!

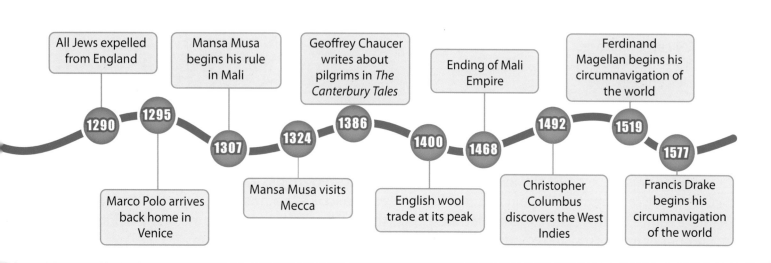

| 1290 | 1295 | 1307 | 1324 | 1386 | 1400 | 1468 | 1492 | 1519 | 1577 |

All Jews expelled from England — 1290

Mansa Musa begins his rule in Mali — 1307

Geoffrey Chaucer writes about pilgrims in *The Canterbury Tales* — 1386

Ending of Mali Empire — 1468

Ferdinand Magellan begins his circumnavigation of the world — 1519

Marco Polo arrives back home in Venice — 1295

Mansa Musa visits Mecca — 1324

English wool trade at its peak — 1400

Christopher Columbus discovers the West Indies — 1492

Francis Drake begins his circumnavigation of the world — 1577

What was the impact of Arab culture in the Middle Ages?

In this lesson you will:

- find out about how Arabs traded and travelled

- describe features of life in the Arab world.

Travel and trade in the Arab world

In the Middle Ages, Arab traders travelled far and wide buying and selling goods. As a result, a number of Arabic words entered into other languages including English.

Think about it

1 a) Below is a table with Arabic words and a clue to the English word that comes from it. Copy and complete the table and work out what each Arabic word means.

Arabic word	Clue	English
Súkkar	Used to make things sweet	
al-kohl	A strong drink	
amir-al-bahr	The person in charge of the navy	
Laimum	A bitter fruit	
Zarafah	An animal with a very long neck	
Hashshashin	Someone who kills (assassinates) another person	
Mūmīya	A wrapped up dead body	
Matrah	Something you lie on when in bed	
Qutn	A material used to make clothes	

What was the extent of Arab trade?

Goods were carried across the Arab world by sea or overland by caravan. This was not the kind of caravan you might think of. In medieval times, it was a collection of camels, sometimes hundreds of them, which carried goods.

At the centre of the Islamic world was the city of Baghdad. By the beginning of the ninth century, Baghdad was the biggest city in the world. One of the reasons it was so big was that it was a centre for trade. Across Baghdad were a number of markets selling goods such as fruit

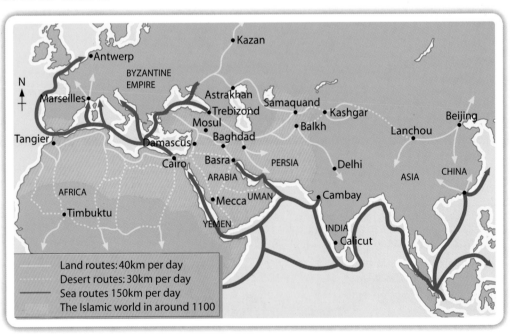

Land routes: 40km per day
Desert routes: 30km per day
Sea routes 150km per day
The Islamic world in around 1100

and flowers, books, gold and many other items. Have a look at **sources a** (a Baghdad trade list from the ninth century) and **b** (some of the belongings of Baghdad's ruler, the Caliph).

a

*From India: tigers, elephants, rubies,
sandalwood and coconuts.*
*From China: spices, silk, porcelain, paper, ink,
spirited horses, saddles and rhubarb.*
*From the Byzantines: silver and gold vessels,
coins, medicines, cloth, slave-girls, experts in
water engineering and farming.*
*From Arabia: horses, pedigree she-camels,
tanned hides.*
From North Africa: leopards and black falcons.
*From the Yemen: cloaks, giraffes, breastplates,
indigo.*
From Egypt: donkeys, fine cloth.
*From Central Asia: slaves, armour, helmets,
grapes, sugarcane.*
*From Persia: Plums, soft woollen coats, honey,
fruit drinks, glass.*

■ *Baghdad trade list, a ninth-century
guide to imports to Baghdad.*

Your turn ...

1 b) Using the map and **sources a** and **b**, pretend you are
a Baghdad merchant buying and selling goods from
across the world. You want to advertise your goods.
Design a poster that shows what you have for sale and
stresses that your trade links extend far and wide.

Mecca

Most people in the Arab world were followers of Islam.
Followers of Islam are called Muslims. Founded by the
Prophet Mohammed in the seventh century, he instructed
that all Muslims should make the pilgrimage to the holy
city of Mecca at least once in their lives (see pages 140–
141). Many rich pilgrims would bring a large number of
gifts with them which they would give out on their way
to Mecca. **Sources c** and **d** give examples.

b

4,000 embroidered robes
4,000 silk cloaks
2,000 pairs of trousers
4,000 turbans
500,000 gold coins
5,000 cushions
1,000 washbasins
300 stoves
4,000 pairs of socks
1,000 Armenian carpets

■ *Some of the Caliph's
belongings, 809.*

c

■ *The pilgrimage of the Prophet Ali, from a
nineteenth century Persian manuscript*

d

*Jamila brought with her,
loaded on camels, fresh
green vegetables contained
in earthenware crocks. She
brought 500 horses and
camels for disabled pilgrims
to ride on. She gave 10,000
dinars to the **Ka'bah**. She
freed 300 slaves and 200
slave-girls. She provided
50,000 fine robes for the
ordinary people in Mecca.*

■ *An account
of the
pilgrimage
of Jamila
bint Nasir in
977.*

Over to you...

2 Pilgrims and travellers would stop for
the night at hostels that were known as
caravanserais. Use all the information on
the map and the sources in this lesson
to understand what it's like to be a
pilgrim and a merchant. Working with a
partner, one of should take the role of a
pilgrim, the other a merchant. These are
the types of things you might discuss.

● How you travel.

● What you have with you.

● Where you have come from and
where you are going.

Travel diary

3 Imagine that you are
writing a page of a
pilgrim's or a merchant's
travel diary. Describe life
on the road. You might
include the following
information in your extract.

● Distances travelled.

● Other travellers.

● What you have seen
on the road.

Key words

Ka'bah
The building towards which
Muslims face five times every
day in prayer.

In this lesson you will:

- learn about Arab inventions and discoveries that influenced Europe in the Middle Ages

- explain how Arab ideas influenced Europe.

Arab science and medicine

It is not just people who travel. Ideas and inventions travelled up and down the trade routes along with the goods. The influence of the Arab world on European ideas throughout the Middle Ages was huge.

Arabic numerals

The Arabs led the world in mathematics in the Middle Ages. In the ninth century, the Persian mathematician Al-Khwarizmi introduced a clear numbering system. People in Europe used Roman numerals and it was not until the introduction of the printing press in the fifteenth century that Arabic numbers caught on.

? *Can you do these sums?*

III + VII   IX + VIII   XII + XVI   5 + 8   9 + 10   11 + 12

The information in this table might help.

Arabic numbers	1	2	3	4	5	6	7	8	9	10	11	12	13	14	15
Roman numbers	I	II	III	IV	V	VI	VII	VIII	IX	X	XI	XII	XIII	XIV	XV

Arabic numbering is an example of just one idea that spread from the Arab world to Europe in the Middle Ages. Here are some more examples.

■ *This sixteenth century painting shows workers at the observatory of Muradd III in Istanbul*

A The astrolabe

The astrolabe was first written about by the Greeks and Romans. They understood that it was possible to tell the time and work out direction and location when travelling by measuring distances from the planets and stars.

The astrolabe was first used in the Arab world in the eighth century. Muslims found it useful because it told them the prayer times and also the direction of Mecca.

Europeans began to buy astrolabes in the eleventh century. In the thirteenth century, astrolabes were used by European travellers and sailors.

■ *An astrolabe is a disc with the edge marked in degrees and a pointer. It was invented to help people tell the time and to work out direction and location.*

By foot
Most peasants could not afford any form of animal transport, so they walked.

By carriage
Ladies travelled in carriages covered in painted cloth (you can see what these looked like in 3.11– see **source a**).

How did people travel?

Pulling a cart
Many peasants pulled small two-wheeled carts full of straw or hay. Richer peasants could afford oxen to pull their cart to market.

By horse
By far the fastest means of transport those who could afford it was a horse. Horses could travel across country, through woods and used tracks, and avoid the roads.

By packhorse
This was a common way to carry heavy or bulky good such as bundles of wool.

What problems did people face?

Poor state of the roads
The roads had not been improved since Roman times. They were often just dirt tracks that turned into mud when it rained and they were full of potholes.

Blocked roads
The road could often be blocked by falling trees, flooding or landslides of rocks and mud.

Night time
Most travellers dare not travel by night for fear of bandits and robbers.

Slow traffic
People were often held up by slow carts or wagons making their way to market.

Discomfort
Travelling in a carriage or cart was uncomfortable: there were no springs, no suspension and the roads were very bumpy.

Robbers and bandits
The countryside was full of woods and forests in which bandits lived.

Stop overs

Abbeys and monasteries
All religious houses would have accommodation for tired travellers.

Hedges
Those with no money would have to sleep under a hedge.

Inns
In towns and also by the roadside, travellers could get a meal, a bed and fresh horses (if needed).

Castles
Castles would give a traveller somewhere to sleep for the night: for the rich it was a proper bed, for the poor a pile of hay.

Take a journey

1   You are going to tell the story of a medieval journey. Your first job is to pick a traveller from the bottom of this page. Then you need to choose the following to match your chosen traveller:

- a destination/reason for travel
- means of transport
- problems you might face
- stop-over point (if you have one)
- arrival.

Write the story

2   Now, using the chosen information, write a short story of your journey. You might also want to illustrate your story.

What are the similarities and differences?

3   Some things about travel in the Middle Ages are very different from travel today but some things are very similar.

   a) Think of two similarities between travel in the Middle Ages and today.

   b) Think of two differences between travel in the Middle Ages and today.

Here are some travellers for you to meet.

| A pilgrim | A peasant | A lady | A monk | A merchant |

In this lesson you will:

- find out about robbers and bandits in medieval England

- use evidence in an enquiry.

Robbers and bandits

? *Look at this picture. What do you think has happened here?*

Solve the crime

Travelling on roads between towns and villages in medieval England was especially difficult because of the activities of robbers and bandits. They would hide in the woods or forest close to the roads and would surprise passing travellers. In the thirteenth century the situation had got so bad that in 1285 the Statute of Winchester was issued by Parliament. This made landowners clear the forest for 60 metres either side of the road outside market towns. By the fifteenth century this law was being ignored and travelling on the roads had, again, become very dangerous indeed.

Look at the evidence

1 It is clear from looking at the murder scene that a crime has been committed. You are the local sheriff. You get to the scene of the crime first. It is your job to find out as much as you can about what has happened.

First you need to identify your evidence. Make a list and perhaps draw all of the pieces of evidence found at the crime scene.

Exhibit 1:
Map

Exhibit 2:
Further items
found at the scene

Servant John Smith has reported his master William Tresham as missing. His master was due back from Northampton yesterday. Tresham's visit to Northampton had been a secret so he had travelled alone. Smith had kept the secret about Tresham's journey. However, he had mentioned to a man he met in the Swan Inn a week ago that he would be able to play cards on 22 September because his master was leaving Moulton early in the morning on that day to go to an important meeting.

Exhibit 3:
Missing person
report

20 August 1450

Dear William

Thank you for your letter. I will be travelling through Northamptonshire on my way to see my cousin the king. I have been five years in Ireland and have heard the news of the growing violence in England.

As Speaker of the House of Commons, you are a very important man. I would like to meet you in Northampton on 22 September so that you can tell me about the recent events. I am particularly interested to hear about the roadside murder in May of the king's chief adviser, William Pole.

I would also like to know more about the revolt led by Jack Cade. It is amazing that he managed to take control of London in June. England has lost control of Normandy this month and many people are unhappy with the king. I am going to London to tell him what the people think of him.

Stay safe and do not tell people of your movements. These are violent times. Please bring this letter with you to our meeting as proof of your identity.

Yours,

Richard of York

Exhibit 5:
Physician's Report

The body was covered in stab wounds and the person's throat had been cut.

Consider the evidence

2 Using all of the evidence, you are to report on what happened. In your account you need to cover the following points:

- the identity of the murder victim
- the events surrounding the murder.

In conclusion

3 What does the evidence of this lesson and Lesson 3.2a tell you about travel in medieval England? Which four points of conclusion would you make?

3.2c

Taking it further!

Shipwrecks

One of the easiest and quickest ways to travel in the Middle Ages was by water, either by river or by sea. But, like roads, water travel also had its dangers. At sea, pirates lay in wait for ships. They would seize cargos and sell anyone they found on board into slavery. Ships also sank in storms with everything lost.

Many of these sunken ships still sit at the bottom of the seabed. They can give us huge amounts of evidence about the past. But sometime wrecks hold on board huge amounts of treasure. Here is the problem: often when getting to the treasure other evidence is destroyed.

Below is the story of a recent discovery of a treasure ship, plus the reactions of a treasure hunter and an archaeologist. Read through all three, then look at the discussion point.

Newspaper story

A fortune beyond the imagination of any pirate of the Caribbean has been discovered in the dangerous seas off the Scilly Isles: 17 tonnes of gold and silver coins – 500,000 in all. The company that found the treasure, Marine Exploration, said yesterday it believed the coins were worth an average of £500 each, giving a total estimated value of £250 million.

The treasure hunter

The gold and silver coins are in excellent condition. We think that all coin collectors will be very excited about this find. We are in this business to make money. One of the next ships we are looking for is *HMS Sussex*, an English ship that sank in a storm off Gibraltar and said to be carrying 9 tonnes of gold coins. Another ship for us to find is the French *Notre Dame de Deliverance*, which sank in a hurricane shortly after leaving Cuba, with a cargo said to include 17 chests of gold bullion, six chests of gems and more than a million pieces of silver – together perhaps worth over US$1 billion.

Archaeologist

WE NEED TO PROTECT HISTORIC WRECKS. NEW TECHNOLOGY MEANS THAT MORE AND MORE WRECKS ARE BEING FOUND AND SEARCHED. WHEN THE TREASURE HUNTERS GET TO A SHIP THEY DESTROY THE SITE IN SEARCH OF THE TREASURE. WE WANT TO RECORD, PRESERVE AND THEN PUBLISH DETAILS ABOUT ALL OF THE OTHER ARTEFACTS AT THE SITE. INSTEAD THEY USE GREAT SCOOPING MACHINES TO DIG UP THE TREASURE INTO GREAT SKIPS. A MASS OF HISTORICAL EVIDENCE IS BEING LOST FOR EVER FROM THESE SITES.

Discuss...

1. What is more important: finding the treasure or preserving the historical evidence?

2. Should treasure hunters be allowed to recover treasure without any care being shown towards the other historical evidence?

3. What rules would you make treasure hunters follow?

Next Lesson

In this lesson you will:

- **find out where Christians went on pilgrimages**

- **discover what Geoffrey Chaucer had to say about pilgrims.**

Who went on pilgrimages and where did they go?

All sorts of different people went on pilgrimages in the Middle Ages and they went for a variety of reasons. They went:

- to make amends for a sin they had confessed to a priest
- because they wanted to be rewarded in heaven

- to reduce the time their soul would spend in purgatory
- in the hope that a miracle would happen
- to show that they were good people.

Where rich people went

Rich people travelled the furthest. This was because they could afford to take time out to go to far away holy places such as Rome and even Jerusalem.

Where poor people went

Poorer people made pilgrimages to a local **shrine** close to where they lived. If they could afford it they might go further to a national shrine such as Walsingham or Canterbury.

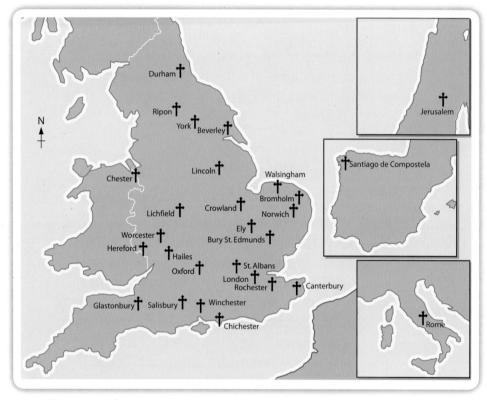

■ *These maps show some of the holy places that Christians might have visited on pilgrimage.*

Where women went

At the start of this period not many women went on pilgrimages, and all sorts of difficulties were put in their way. For example, they had to ask permission from their husband, father or abbot before they could make such a journey. It was not acceptable for women to travel alone. Complicated arrangements had to be made for suitable men to accompany them. But women were keen to visit shrines and gradually it became acceptable for women to make pilgrimages within England.

○ **Key words**

Shrine
A holy place, usually associated with an important religious person.

Where people travelled on pilgrimages

Your turn ...

1 Can you guess where these people might have gone on a pilgrimage?
- A rich wool merchant, living in Long Melford, Suffolk.
- A poor agricultural labourer working on estates in Selby, North Yorkshire.
- A prosperous boat builder living in Polperro, Cornwall.
- A stonemason who travels the country, working on cathedrals.
  You might need a modern atlas to help you!

The Canterbury Tales

In about 1386, a poet called Geoffrey Chaucer wrote a poem called *The Canterbury Tales*. It is really a story about twelve people who went on a pilgrimage to to the shrine of Saint Thomas Becket in Canterbury Cathedral. The story tells some of the adventures the pilgrims had on the way; here are some of them.

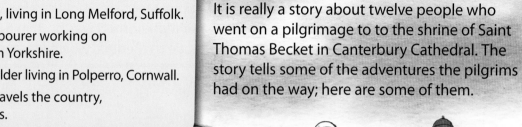

a
Wide was his parish, with houses far apart,
Yet he neglected not in rain or thunder,
In sickness or in grief, to pay a call
On the remotest, whether great or small.

b
He was an honest worker, good and true.
For steadily about his work he went
To thrash his corn, to dig or to manure
Or make a ditch; and he would help the poor
For love of Christ and never take a penny.

c
Many's the meal you have sold
That has been twice warmed up and twice left cold.
Many a pilgrim's cursed you more than once
When suffering the effects of your stale food.

d
The cause of every illness you'd got
He knew, whether dry, cold, moist or hot.
All his apothecaries in a tribe
Were ready with the drugs he would prescribe.
Gold stimulates the heart, or so we're told.
He therefore had a special love of gold.

e
A worthy woman all her life
She'd had five husbands, married them all.
And she had been three times to Jerusalem,
Seen many strange rivers and passed over them;
She'd been to Rome and also to Bologne,
St James of Compostela and Cologne.

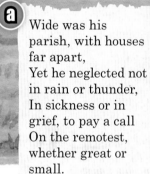

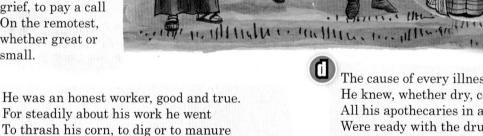

Match make!

2 Look at the illustrations and read **sources a–e**.
  a) Can you match Chaucer's descriptions to the pilgrims in the illustration? How can you be sure?
  b) Can we trust Chaucer to give us a true picture of people who went on Christian pilgrimages? Why?

Argue a case

3 Work with a partner. Each of you must choose to be one of Chaucer's pilgrims. Try to convince the other person that your reasons for going on a pilgrimage were far better than theirs.

Muslim pilgrimages

All Muslims are expected to make a pilgrimage, called a Hajj, to Mecca at least once in their lifetime. Mecca is a holy city for Muslims because that was where the Prophet Mohammed was born in 570. Many Muslims also aim to make a pilgrimage to Medina, which is where Mohammed died.

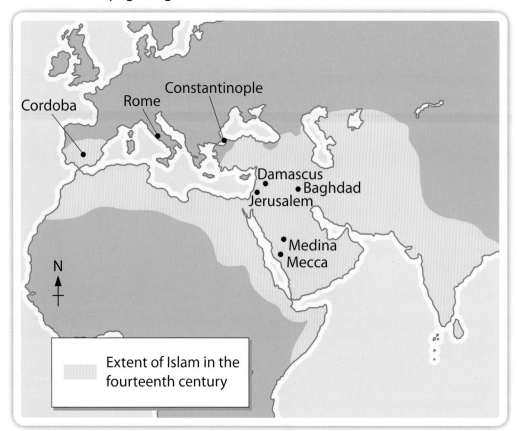

Extent of Islam in the fourteenth century

Think about it

1 What sort of problems would pilgrims face as they travelled to Mecca from all over the Islamic world? Work with a partner and make a list. Compare your list with those others have made and create a whole class list.

If getting to Mecca was so difficult, why did Muslims go?

Writing a rihla

The journeys that many pilgrims made were, as you have discovered, long and difficult. Some pilgrims wrote travel journals, called rihlas, in which they wrote down their impressions of the countries through which they travelled. Some pilgrims jotted down things as they travelled; others wrote up their Hajj afterwards. Rihlas don't all agree with each other and some tell very funny stories. One of the longest, and most famous, rihlas was that written in the 1300s about Ibn Battuta's travels.

Who was Ibn Battuta?

Ibn Battuta was born in Morocco in 1304. When he was 21 years old he set out on his Hajj to Mecca.

Reaching Mecca in 1326, he could have stayed for a while and then gone home to carry on his work as a lawyer. Instead, he decided to travel. He went nearly everywhere in the then known world: Russia and India, Africa and China as well as the lands around the Mediterranean Sea.

He travelled approximately 121,000 kilometres! When he finally got back to Morocco in 1354, the Sultan was so impressed that he got a young scholar, called Ibn Juzayy, to write down everything Ibn Battuta told him about his travels.

These are some of the things he said about his Hajj, his pilgrimage to Mecca.

On 1 September 1326, the Hijaz caravan left Damascus and I set off along with it. The great camel caravan halted at Tabuk for four days to rest and to give water to the camels. The water-carriers camp beside the spring and they have tanks made of buffalo hides, like great cisterns, from which they water the camels and fill the waterskins.

al-'Ula is a large and pleasant village with palm-gardens and water-springs. The pilgrims halt there for four days to stock up with provisions and wash their clothes. The Christian merchants of Syria may come as far as this and no further. They trade in provisions and other goods with the pilgrims.

Our stay at Medina lasted four days. We spent every night in the splendid mosque where the people, after forming circles in the courtyard and lighting large numbers of candles, would pass the time reciting from the Koran or chanting, or visiting the holy tomb.

We halted 8 kilometres from Mecca. Here I took off my tailored clothes, bathed and put on the pilgrim's robe. I prayed and dedicated myself to the pilgrimage.

The people of Mecca have many excellent qualities. They are generous to the humble and weak, and are kind to strangers. When any one of them makes a feast, he gives first to the pilgrims who are poor and without resources.

Sort it out

2 Write the title: *Ibn Battuta's Hajj*. Draw two columns underneath the title. Head one column 'Religious' and the other 'Non-religious'.

Read carefully through each of Ibn Battuta's extracts, then decide what he said that were about the religious aspects of the Hajj, and the non-religions aspects. The first two have been done for you.

Religious	Non-religious
In Medina he spent every night in the mosque.	He travelled on a camel.

How useful is Ibn Battuta's rihla?

3 Below are a number of statements about Ibn Battuta's rihla.

- It was written down nearly 30 years after he began his travels.
- It was not written down by Ibn Battuta himself, but dictated by him to a scribe.
- Some of the descriptive passages are borrowed from other people's rihlas.
- Ibn Battuta did not take part in all the events he describes.

Does this mean that Ibn Battuta's rihla is no use to historians trying to find out what the Islamic world was like in the fourteenth century? Explain your answer.

Next Lesson

In this lesson you will:

- find out why Jerusalem was such an important city

- use the sources to discover why people went on Crusades.

Going on a Crusade

Take a look at the Crusader in **source a**.

■ *Image of a young Crusader, from the Westminster Psalter, 1175*

Your turn ...

1 What word would you use to describe this young man? Thoughtful? Serious? Happy? Angry? Sad? War-like? Write two sentences:

- one saying what impression this picture gives you

- the other saying why you get this impression.

Compare what you have written with others in your class. Have you all got the same ideas about this young man?

The young man in **source a** was setting off to fight for Christian control of Jerusalem.

Why was control of Jerusalem important?

For Christians, Jews and Muslims, Jerusalem was a holy city. There were, and still are, important shrines and sites that are central to all these religions.

Key words

Crusade
A Christian military expedition made with the aim of recovering Jerusalem from the Muslims.

Holy Land
The region on the eastern shore of the Mediterranean which Christians, Jews and Muslims all treat as important to their religions.

Infidel
The name given to someone of a different religion from one's own.

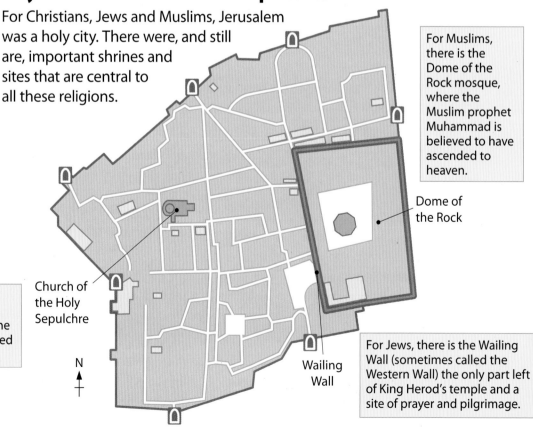

For Muslims, there is the Dome of the Rock mosque, where the Muslim prophet Muhammad is believed to have ascended to heaven.

Dome of the Rock

For Christians, the Church of the Holy Sepulchre built on the site of what is believed to be Christ's tomb.

Church of the Holy Sepulchre

Wailing Wall

For Jews, there is the Wailing Wall (sometimes called the Western Wall) the only part left of King Herod's temple and a site of prayer and pilgrimage.

N

For centuries, Christians, Jews and Muslims had lived more or less peacefully in the same city. But by 1087 the Muslim Turks had taken over most of the **Holy Land**. Travel to Jerusalem was becoming impossible for anyone except Muslims. The Pope, Urban II, decided to act. He didn't like the Muslim takeover of land and he didn't like the threat Muslims were posing to Christianity. In 1095 he made a speech to the Christian rulers of Western Europe, given in **source b**.

Thousands of people responded to Pope Urban's call, not just kings and lords but soldiers and ordinary people anxious to help. And so the First **Crusade** began.

*I speak as a messenger from God. You must hasten to help your brothers in the East. The Turkish Muslims have seized more and more of the lands of the Christians, have defeated them seven times in many battles, killed or captured many people, destroyed churches and devastated the kingdom of God. In the name of God, I beg you to drive out these foul creatures. Set out for Jerusalem. Take the land from the wicked **infidel** and make it your own. If you die on the journey or in battle, your sins will be forgiven immediately. God Himself has given me the power to say this.*

■ *From Pope Urban II's speech, 1095.*

Over to you …

2 Read through **source b**, then answer the questions.
   a) Why do you think the Pope mentioned God so often?
   b) What crimes did he accuse the Muslims of committing?
   c) How did he encourage Christians to join the Crusade?

Pope Urban's speech wasn't the only reason people went on Crusades. **Sources c** and **d** suggest other reasons.

Many have gone on Crusades to escape from their own land. There are criminals, thieves, robbers, pirates, dice-players, men who have left their wives and women who have left their husbands.

■ *Written by a French priest in the thirteenth century.*

My dear wife, I now have twice as much silver, gold and other riches as I had when I set off on this Crusade.

■ *Written by a French Crusader to his wife, in the thirteenth century.*

In conclusion …

3 Work in pairs. You are going to have a furious quarrel! You can be husband and wife, brother and sister, mother and son, father and son or two friends. It doesn't matter. You choose! One of you wants to go on a Crusade and the other wants to stop the person going on a Crusade.

Use all the information in this lesson to create both sides of the argument.

Write out the argument. Remember to start by being reasonable and end up in a furious temper. Remember, too, to keep the argument medieval. You can't take your mobile phone with you to keep in touch!

The First Crusade 1095–1099

The Crusader force was about 30,000 strong as it swept through Europe on its way to Jerusalem. It had no overall commander and was really a collection of small armies all with one purpose in mind: to recapture Jerusalem for Christianity. The journey overland was dangerous. Crusaders had to cope with attacks from Muslims, with disease and with homesickness.

? *Look at this map. What can we learn about the First Crusade from it?*

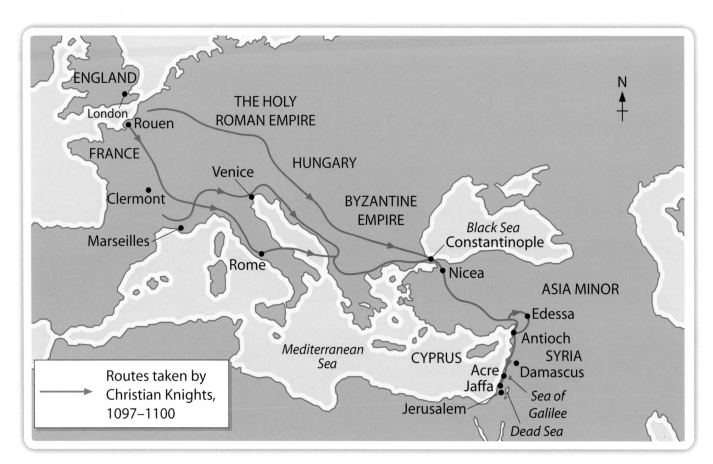

Routes taken by Christian Knights, 1097–1100

- *Map to show the different routes taken by the crusaders to get to the Holy Land on the First Crusade.*

Use the map

1 Look at the map above.

   a) What does it tell you about where the Crusading armies came from?

   b) Why do you think the Crusaders didn't travel to Jerusalem by sea, which would at least have been quicker?

Battles on the way

On the way to Jerusalem, the Crusaders attacked and captured the cities of Nicea in May 1097 and Antioch in June 1098. They set up a Crusader state in Edessa and gradually became more confident that they could take the prize of Jerusalem!

 This picture shows part of the siege of Nicea in 1097. It was painted by Guillaume de Tyr in the eleventh century.

The Siege of Jerusalem, July 1099

On arrival outside Jerusalem's city walls, the Crusaders' chances of taking the city didn't look good. Their **siege** equipment hadn't arrived! It took three weeks before the battering rams and siege towers caught up with the Crusaders, who desperately wanted to use them. To make matters worse, the defending Muslims had collected as much food as they could from the villages outside the city walls and stored it inside the city. They had enough supplies to keep them going for weeks, while the attacking Crusaders had very little to live on.

The Muslims started a rumour, too, that they had poisoned the wells. Many Crusaders were afraid to drink the local water. And in the July heat this was quite a problem.

The Muslims inside Jerusalem prepared to defend the city. They packed the walls on the city side with straw bales to absorb the impact of battering rams. They massed great vats of oil to set alight and pour down on the attackers. They were ready! But they lost. Finally, the Crusaders managed to break through Jerusalem's city walls using their sophisticated siege equipment.

 **Key words**

Siege
Attempt to force a town or a castle to surrender by surrounding it.

b

The storming of Jerusalem, from a fourteenth century French manuscript.

Source b is a picture from a fourteenth-century French manuscript showing how the crusaders stormed Jerusalem.

Once successfully inside the gates, the Crusaders ran riot. They destroyed the holy Muslim site of the Dome on the Rock and slaughtered nearly 70,000 people who were in Jerusalem. **Source c** is what a Crusader who was in Jerusalem at the time wrote.

c

Our men chased the defenders, killing as many as they could until they were up to their ankles in blood. When our men captured the Temple they killed whoever they wished. Soon our soldiers took the whole city and seized gold, silver and houses full of treasure. Those Muslims who had survived were forced to collect the bodies. The dead Muslims were piled up high outside the city and their bodies burned.

Written by a crusader who was in Jerusalem at the time.

Over to you ...

2 If you had been in charge of the City of Jerusalem, how would you have defended it so that the Crusaders didn't get in?

Work with a partner. You will need to think about:

- what the Muslims did that worked, and try to improve on those tactics
- what the Muslims didn't do but which could have worked
- how the Crusaders did get in
- what the Muslims could have done to stop them.

In conclusion ...

3 Look back at **source a** in Lesson 3.4a – the picture of the young Crusader. Are you surprised that he would have behaved, once inside Jerusalem, in the way described?

The Crusaders must have felt victorious. They had captured Jerusalem and, so they believed, made it safe for Christians for all time. In the years that followed, thousands of Crusaders flooded into the Holy Land, especially from France, and settled down. They built castles to protect themselves, their families and their newly conquered lands.

Taking it further!

Who was Salah al-Deen?

In 1171 a new Muslim leader, Salah al-Deen, came to power in Egypt. He swept through the Holy Land, defeating Crusaders as he went. Finally, in October 1187 he captured Jerusalem. Although he allowed Christians and Jews to worship freely, the Christian world was horrified and its leaders, including King Richard I of England, launched the Third Crusade (1189–1192) with the aim of retaking Jerusalem. But Salah al-Deen defended Jerusalem well and the Crusaders failed to take the city.

Historians disagree, so see what you think of him after reading **sources a–d** – all written in Salah al-Deen's time.

a

God – may He be honoured and glorified – gave the upper hand to the Sultan Salah al-Din. God made straight for the Sultan the road leading to his enemies' destruction. If his only achievement was this one victory then he would still be above all the kings of former times, let alone those of his own age.

■ *Written by Imad ad-Din al-Isfahahani, about the Battle of Hattin, which took place in 1187. Imad ad-Din al-Isfahahani was Salah al-Deen's secretary.*

b

*So many were killed, so many made prisoner that even the enemy felt sorry for our people. Some of the prisoners were kept safe until Salah al-Deen decided what to do with them. Among them was Reynald of Chatillon. The tyrant, Salah al-Deen, cut off his proud head with his own hands. This was either because he was in a rage, or possibly out of respect for so great a man. All the **Templars** who were captured he ordered to be beheaded. He was determined to wipe them out for he knew they were stronger than him in battle.*

■ *Written by an English monk in 1200, also about the Battle of Hattin.*

c

I never saw him find the enemy too powerful. He would think carefully about each aspect of the situation and take the necessary steps to deal with it, without becoming angry. At the Battle of Acre, the centre of the Muslim army was broken, but he stood firm with a handful of men and led them into battle again.

■ *Written by one of Salah al-Deen's officials about his military skills.*

d

During a siege of one of the towns, one of the European women came to us asking to see Salah al-Din. She said that her daughter had been taken by Muslims in the night. Tears came to Salah al-Deen's eyes and he sent a horseman to the local slave market to look for the girl. He returned soon after with her, safe. The girl's mother threw herself to the floor with emotion.

■ *Written by a Muslim, Baha ad-Din Ibn Shaddad, about one of Salah al-Deen's sieges.*

Key words

Templar
A member of a religious military order founded in Jerusalem about 1118.

Give an opinion

1 Read **sources a–d**. What do you think of Salah al-Deen? Was he a cruel tyrant or a brilliant military leader? What evidence will you use from these sources to back up your opinion?

2 Compare your ideas with those written by someone else in your class. Do you agree with their answers? Can you think of reasons for any agreement or disagreement?

Next Lesson

Why did some empires grow in the Middle Ages?

The Mali Empire

An empire is a collection of countries that have been conquered and are ruled by one state. One of the greatest empires the world has ever seen was the Mali Empire. It lasted from 1235 to 1468. It covered much of West Africa and was known throughout the world for its great wealth.

? *Here are two pieces of evidence about the Mali Empire. Look at them both. What can you see?*

■ *Map from 1375 showing Mansa Musa, the King of Mali, holding a gold nugget.*

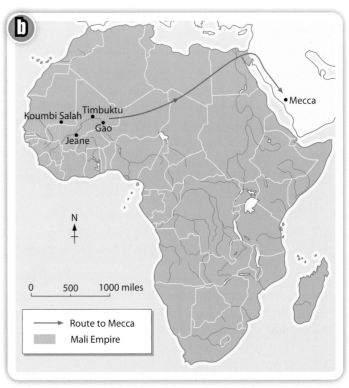

■ *A modern map of the Mali Empire, showing it's extent in c.1350.*

Why was the Mali Empire so strong?

History detective

This lesson is about the Mali Empire. Use books or the Internet to find out about any other empires.

Read and think

1 Read through the factors opposite.
   a) Discuss with a partner how important you think each factor was in helping the Mali Empire to become strong.
   b) Now draw a pyramid shape on a piece of paper and place these factors on it. Put the ones you think were most important at the top and the least important at the bottom.

THE FACTORS

Conquest

The Mali Empire was created through battle. In around 1235, the leader of Keita tribe, Sundiata, led an army against the might of the Sosso kingdom of Kaniaga. Sundiata's troops were victorious. The new empire of Mali was born in battle. Because of his skill and bravery, Sundiata became known as the 'Lion King'.

Emperor

The rulers of the Mali Empires became known as Mansa, or Emperor. The most famous Mansa was Mansa Musa who ruled the Mali Empire between 1307 and 1332. He made the empire even stronger by bringing in more cities and states under his rule. At one point the Mali Empire covered more territory than the whole of Europe.

Trade

Under Sundiata, Mali gained control of the region's gold and salt trade. All gold mined in the Mali empire belonged to the Mansa. There were three great gold mines in Mali which produced huge amounts of gold. It was not just gold that was a source of wealth. The Mali Empire grew on the back of trade in goods that included cotton, copper and salt.

Rules

The Mali Empire was governed under one set of rules. All tribes sent representatives to a Great Assembly. At the assembly they would discuss the rules, such as how slaves should be looked after.

Wealth

Mansa Musa was a Muslim, so in 1324 he went on a visit to Mecca, the holy city of Islam. On his journey to and from Mecca he spent huge amounts of gold. He was so rich that he could afford to take thousands of people with him on pilgrimage.

Army

The Mali Empire was defended by an army of 100,000 soldiers. These soldiers could be called on at any moment to defend the empire.

C

■ *An example of wood carving from the Mali Empire, fifteenth Century.*

Summarise the empire

2 Use your pyramid to explain, in no more than 100 words, why the Mali Empire was so strong. Because you do not have many words to use, you will have to choose what information you will leave in and what to leave out.

Why top?

3 Which factor have you chosen to sit on the top of your pyramid? Why have you chosen it? Explain your reasons to people in another group, then hear what they have put on top.

In this lesson you will:

■ find out reasons for the growth of the Ottoman Empire

■ identify and link causes together.

The Ottoman Empire

Look carefully at the map below, which shows the extent of the Ottoman Empire in 1566.

? *Imagine that you are describing this empire to someone who has not seen the map. What points would you make?*

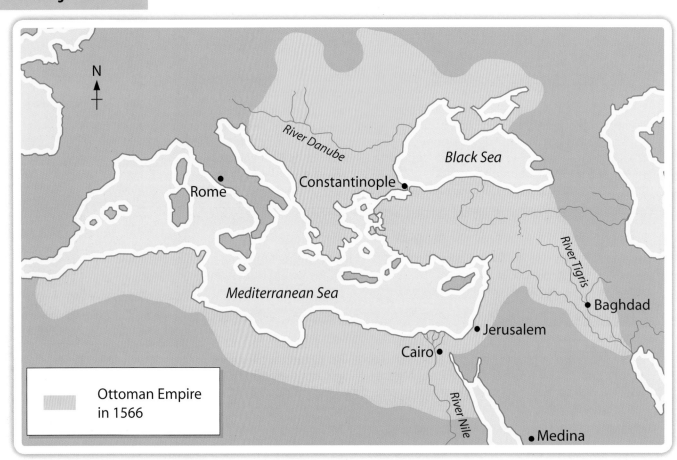

Ottoman Empire in 1566

Make connections

1 Carefully read through what historians **A–E** say. Then match the historian to one of these reasons:

   i) leadership

   ii) military conquest

   iii) weakness of others

   iv) religion

   v) tolerance.

In Lesson 3.5a you found out why the Mali Empire grew and stayed strong. Many of the same reasons could be used to explain the growth of the Ottoman Empire. From 1300 the Ottoman Turks built an empire that lasted until the twentieth century. As you can see from the map, by the 1560s the Ottoman Empire was very large indeed.

What do the historians tell us?

Historians can be useful sources of information when we want to find out about the past. Here we have the views of some historians on the Ottoman Empire. Between them they give five main reasons for the growth of the Ottoman Empire.

Historian A

Europe in the fourteenth century was weakened by disease. The Black Death killed one-quarter of the people in Europe. The Europeans were also divided. This meant they were too weak to resist the advance of the Ottoman army up to the gates of Vienna.

Historian B

Early Ottoman leaders and followers were Muslim warriors. Their desire to spread the Muslim faith was one reason why they conquered other people's lands.

Historian C

The Ottomans always had a very strong army with fierce soldiers called Janissaries. These soldiers were not allowed to marry or own any property. Instead they were devoted to fighting. The Ottoman army also used advanced weapons like cannons.

Historian D

The Ottoman Empire was led by Sultans, the first being Osman, or Othman (he is who they got the name 'Ottoman' from). In 1453, Mohammed II captured the great city of Constantinople. He renamed it Istanbul and made it the capital of the Empire. The most famous Ottoman ruler was Suleiman I, who ruled in the period 1520–1566 and whose armies marched into the centre of Europe.

Historian E

The Sultans made some of the laws in the Empire. Other laws were Islamic laws that came from the Koran. The Ottoman rulers allowed non-Muslims to have their own laws and their own courts. They also allowed religious freedom in their Empire. Many types of Christians, such as Greek Orthodox, were very happy under Ottoman rule.

Over to you ...

2 One of the best ways to show you really understand why something happened is to link the views of historians together. Link together, in five points, the ideas of historians **A–E**.

Here is an example:

The link between historians **B** and **E** is that they both mention religion: historian **B** shows how the Ottomans wanted to spread their Muslim faith; historian **E** says Christians in the Ottoman Empire were happy.

Making wider links

3 Look back to the beginning of this enquiry, to lesson 3.5a. What similarities are there between the Ottoman Empire and the Mali Empire? With a partner or in groups, try to make as many links as you can.

What was Great Zimbabwe?

In 1522, a Portuguese writer, João de Barros, reported finding a 'square fortress, of masonry within and without, built of stones of marvellous size' about 48 kilometres inland from the port of Kilwa in East Africa. Further rumours suggested a royal palace where the king and his court ate off gold plates. Barros was, in fact, referring to a huge stone city now known as Great Zimbabwe.

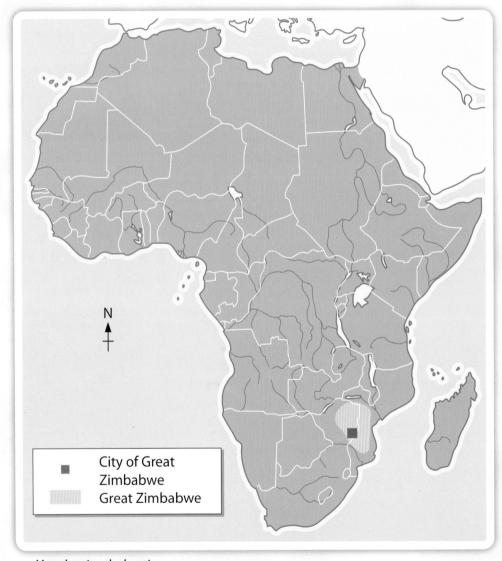

■ *Map showing the location of Great Zimbabwe*

Great Zimbabwe: what we know

Built between 1300 and 1450, the city of Great Zimbabwe was the capital of a trading empire that spread from the Kalahari Desert in the west to the Indian Ocean in the east. The people of Great Zimbabwe were from the Shona tribe. It is possible that they ruled over a huge empire.

From the mid-nineteenth century, a succession of European explorers visited Great Zimbabwe. They made a number of guesses as to who had built the settlement; perhaps it was the Arabs or the Egyptians. They could not accept that Great Zimbabwe was part of a great African civilisation.

Finding out more

Today, we know that Great Zimbabwe was the centre of a rich African empire. The problem for the historian is that the Shona people did not leave much evidence. So we have to rely on a few artefacts plus the views of archaeologists and historians to piece together the evidence. **Sources a–d** show some evidence.

a

■ *Photograph of the Great Enclosure at Great Zimbabwe.*

b

■ *Carved sculptures of birds that might represent the spirit of Zimbabwe's kings, from the fourteenth century.*

c

■ *Modern day African sculptor at work.*

d

In the fourteenth century, Great Zimbabwe controlled gold production on the Zimbabwe Plain. Highly valued items such as gold and imported goods have been found inside the stone enclosures. People were divided into classes: the richer who lived inside the stone enclosure and ate cattle; and the poorer who lived outside the stone enclosures and who ate goat or sheep.

■ *Adapted from Martin Hall and Rebecca Stefoff's* Great Zimbabwe, *written in 2006.*

Draw conclusions ...

From each source (**a–d**), what conclusions can you draw about the African civilisation of Great Zimbabwe? What do these 'things' tell us?

Next Lesson

3.6a

- find out about the goods traded and the trade routes used by English merchants

- work out how to set up as a merchant.

Merchants, trading and trade routes

? *Look at this picture. What's going on?*

Your turn...

1 a) Working in pairs, list all the goods you can see for sale in this busy medieval town market.

b) Now do some intelligent guesswork. Which goods do you think came from abroad? (Keep the list; you will need it later.)

What is a merchant?

In most village markets, people sold the produce they made: cheese and bread, cooking pots and baskets. In towns, it was a bit different. This was because there were **merchants** who had ready-made goods for sale. They bought goods where they were cheap and sold them where they could make a profit. By the 1400s, some merchants were very wealthy, richer than some barons.

? *Look at the map below. Which goods come from abroad?*

Key words

Merchant
Someone who buys and sells goods, but does not make them.

Interest rates
The sum or rate charged for borrowing money.

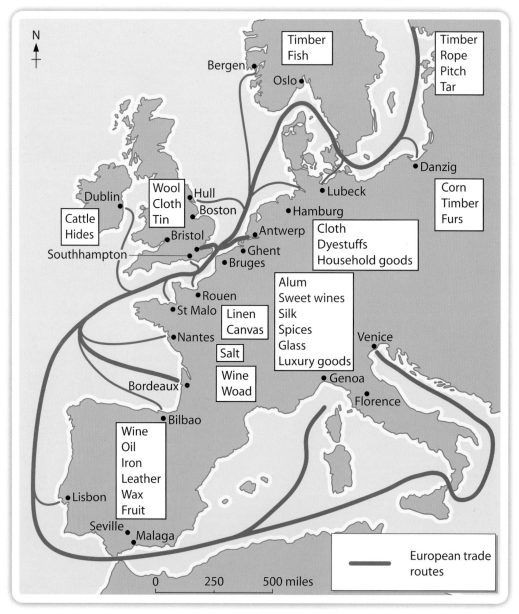

■ *This map shows the main places where medieval merchants traded, c.1450. It also shows the most important goods they traded there.*

Were you correct?

2 Check your list from task 1 against the information on the map. Were you right about which goods were imported from Europe?

What problems did merchants face?

Goods had to be transported overland and, for merchants trading with England, over the sea as well.

■ *Packhorses laden with sacks of grain, from a fifteenth century painting by Sano di Pietro*

Over to you...

2 Look carefully at the paintings in **sources a** and **b**.

   a) Write **two** sentences about each painting. Each sentence should describe **one** problem a merchant transporting goods overland would face. You should end up with four problems!

   b) Think about the problems that merchants would run into when they tried to ship goods by sea. Make a list.

   c) Make a class list of all the problems that merchants might have as they tried to move goods around. Make the list in two columns – one headed 'Land transport', the other 'Sea transport'. Do any problems appear in both columns?

Transporting goods was risky and in order to make money merchants had to be sure that ships and packhorses didn't travel empty in one direction. But merchants had many more problems just transporting goods. They also had to:

- decide which goods they were going to trade in and how they were going to find suppliers
- raise money for their enterprise.

Borrowing money could be tricky. Until the end of the thirteenth century, the only people who were allowed to lend money were the Jews, and they charged high **interest rates**. Many people setting up as merchants sold land to fund their business. But this was risky: if the enterprise failed, then the would-be merchant would have nothing left.

■ *A man being beaten, from 'The Fables of Bidpai', c.1480*

Become a merchant!

3 Work in pairs. You are about to set up as merchants based in England. You must make realistic decisions about what you will do. As you talk through your decisions, draw up a flow chart to show, at each decision point, what you decided. You must answer these questions and you may think of more as you work through the task.

   - Where will you get the money from to fund your enterprise?

   - How will you find out which goods it would be most profitable to buy and sell?

   - Which goods will you buy in England to sell abroad?

   - Which goods will you buy abroad to sell in England?

   - How will you get the goods from your supplier in England to your buyers abroad?

   - How will you get the goods from your supplier abroad to your buyers in England?

   - Is it all worth it? How will you know?

3.6b

In this lesson you will:

- find out about the importance of the wool trade

- work with the sources to discover how wool was shipped abroad.

? *Look at source a. What can you see happening?*

Your turn ...

1 Look carefully at **source a**, a medieval painting.

   a) Write down **three** questions you want to ask about the picture to help you understand what is happening.

   b) Compare your questions with those of the person sitting next to you.

   c) Draw up a class list of the questions you want to ask. (The rest of this lesson should give you the answers to your questions!)

The wool trade

- *Illustration from The French Wars by Ceasar (1474), showing merchants loading wool onto a barge .*

The English wool trade

By the 1400s, wool was the most profitable export from England. English wool was highly prized abroad, where a lot of money was paid for the best fleeces.

Source b shows a letter written by one merchant to another.

b

Right-worshipful sir, I humbly recommend myself to you. My master has shipped his fleeces which you must receive and pay for the transport.

The first ship is the Mary *out of the port of London. William Sordvale is the master. There are seven packs of wool lying aft [behind] the mast. The pack on top is of summer wool; and is marked with an 'O'.*

The next ship is the Christopher *out of Rainham. Harry Wylkyns is the master. He carries seven packs and a half of Cotswold wool lying aft of the mast.*

The third ship is the Thomas *out of Maidstone. Harry Lawson is the master and he brings you six packs of wool. Five packs lyeth before the mast under hatches, and one pack lyeth in the stern.*

Finally there is the Mary *from Rainham. John Danyell is the master. He carries your trunk with your glass and an Essex cheese.*

- *Letter from an English merchant working in England to another English merchant working in Calais, written in 1481.*

Ships like those mentioned in **source b** often sailed together, in a convoy. Sometimes they had fighting ships with them for protection from pirates. **Source c** explains how money was paid to protect a convoy.

c

Paid the sixteenth day of March, for the convoy of wool from the port of London, to William Fethirston, master of the carrack called the King's ship, for the wages of 200 men, every man taking 6s 8d – total £66.13s 4d.

- *The account paid to William Fethirston, who arranged for the protection of a convoy in 1475.*

Because the trade in English wool was so profitable, Parliament tried to make sure that all the wool for export was of good quality, as **source d** shows.

d

Great deceit is done by the owners of wool, who put into the fleeces locks of much worse wool than the top fleece is. They also put tar, stones, sand and dirt inside the fleeces. This angers the buyer and reflects badly on all English merchants. The King has ordered that all wool should be properly packed and, if it is not, a fine of sixpence shall be paid.

- *From a 1463 Act of Parliament about the export of goods from England to other countries.*

Partly because the wool trade was so profitable, many tried their hand at smuggling, as **source e** shows.

e

*That Nicholas Styward, vicar of the church of Rushmere in Suffolk, in a certain creek placed and hid in a certain ship bound for Holland, barrels of wheat and barrels of wool. And that he caused the ship to sail without paying **customs duties** due to the king.*

- *Extract from the records of the Exchequer court.*

● Key words

Customs duties

A tax paid to the government on some goods when they left the country, were brought into the country, and sometimes on both movements of goods.

Over to you ...

2 Look again at **source b**, which gives us a lot of information about the English wool trade.

a) The English merchant is clearly expecting shipments of wool from a number of ports. Which are the ports? Where are they? (You may need to look this up in a modern atlas.)

b) Why do you think the merchant working in England used more than one port from which to ship the wool?

c) Where was the home of the English merchant working in Calais? (Look for clues in **source b**. There's one very strong one!)

d) Why do you think the letter very carefully explains where the wool was stacked that had to be off-loaded at Calais?

In conclusion ...

3 Read sources **c–e**. How could you use them as evidence of the importance of the wool trade? Think about:

- why a ship load of wool would need an armed escort
- why the king would be bothered about some merchants tricking the people who bought wool from them
- why a man as supposedly honest as a vicar would stoop so low as to smuggle wool.

Back to the start

Now think about the big question that began this enquiry: *How important was trade in medieval England?*

Do you now think it was:

- very important
- fairly important
- not very important
- unimportant?

Make your mind up! Find at least two pieces of evidence to back up your decision.

next lesson

Why were the Jews persecuted in the Middle Ages?

How welcome were the Jews in England?

? *Look at source a. What can you see?*

■ *This picture of Jews in England was painted by monks in the early 1300s.*

Ask some questions ...

1 Look carefully at **source a**. All you know about this picture is that:

● it was painted by monks in the early 1300s

● in the early 1300s, Jews had to wear pointed hats or yellow strips on their clothing to show they were Jews.

What questions would you want to ask about the source in order to find out what sort of evidence it provides about Jews in medieval England?

What did the Jews do in England?

Jews were allowed to lend money and to charge interest on the loans. This was very useful to people who needed to borrow money because the Church did not allow Christians to lend money.

Because Jews could charge interest on the loans, some of them became very rich. This meant more money for the royal treasury because rich people were heavily taxed.

The English kings were very grateful for this money and they gave Jews royal protection. Henry I (1100–1135) allowed all Jews to:

● travel throughout England without having to pay tolls

● buy and sell goods and property

● swear oaths on the Jewish holy book, the Torah, rather than the Christian Bible.

But, as **source a** shows, not everything went well for the Jews in England.

Why did things start to go badly for the Jews?

Jewish communities grew in towns including London and Lincoln, York and Norwich. They were often located close to a royal castle where they could get protection if necessary. However, sometimes Christians attacked Jews out of fear, suspicion, jealousy or simply because they were different.

b

Easter:	*borrowed 60 shillings from Vives the Jew of Cambridge for six months and paid 24 shillings interest.*
November:	*Borrowed £3 10s from Jacob of Newport. Kept it 8 months and paid 37 shillings and 4 pence interest.*

■ *From the journals of Richard of Anesty, 1158.*

c

To the Jews, a treacherous nation and enemy of the Christians, King Henry II gave unfair help. This was because of the profits he received from their money lending. He did this so often that the Jews became rude towards the Christians and inflicted great harm on them.

■ *Written by William of Newburgh, a Christian priest, in 1196.*

What do the sources tell us?

2 Look at **sources b** and **c**.
   a) Can you find any clues that might tell you the Jews were doing well?
   b) Can you find any clues that might tell you why people began to turn against the Jews?
   c) Now read **sources d** and **e**. Does anything here surprise you?

d

While the king was seated at table, the chief men of the Jews came to offer presents to him. The day before, this had been forbidden. And so the common people rushed on the Jews, stripped them and cast them forth out of the king's hall. The citizens of London, on hearing this, attacked the Jews in the city and burned their houses. By the kindness of their Christian friends, some few escaped.

■ *Written by Richard of Hovenden, who wrote a history of the reigns of Henry II and Richard I. He died in 1201. Here he is writing about the coronation of Richard I in 1189.*

e

*King John decided that the Jews should pay for the army he wanted to send into Ireland. These unhappy people, whose riches brought them more trouble than their religion, were seized all over the kingdom. They were cruelly treated until they agreed to pay. Abraham, a Jew from Bristol, refused to pay. King John ordered a tooth to be pulled from his mouth every day until he agreed to pay 10,000 **marks**. After losing seven teeth he paid this enormous sum.*

■ *From* The New History of London, *published in 1773. Here the writer is describing an event in 1212.*

In conclusion ...

3 Work in pairs. Imagine you are young Jews who have just settled in England. Most of your family live in Spain.

   a) Each of you should write a letter to your family. One must try to persuade your family to come and settle in England. The other must try to persuade them not to.

Include as much information as you can about life in England for Jews as you try to persuade your family that your view is correct.

   b) Now compare your letters. What has been left out of one but not the other? What has been emphasised in one but not the other? Which letter do you think is the most persuasive and why?

In this lesson you will:

- find out what happened in Clifford's Tower, York, in 1190

- make decisions about why events turned out as they did.

Massacre 1190!

If you visited Clifford's Tower in York today, you would find a stone tower. This is all that is left of a great stone castle that once dominated York. You would also find plenty of tourists, as many tours of York start here.

It all looks peaceful and sunny in **source a**. But in March 1190, something terrible happened here. It was so terrible that people have not forgotten about it through the centuries. The slab you can see in **source b** is set at the base of Clifford's Tower.

> On the night of Friday 16 March 1190 some 150 Jews and Jewesses of York having sought protection in the Royal Castle on this site from a mob incited by Richard Malebisse and others chose to die at each other's hands rather than renounce their faith
>
> שמו לד כבוד ותהלתו באים

Think about it ...

1 Carefully read the wording on the slab in **source b**.

a) Write down **two** questions you would want to ask about the slab and what it says.

b) Compare your questions with those of the person sitting next to you. Do this round the class until you have a complete list of different questions.

What happened on the night of Friday 15 March 1190?

What happened that night was terrible. As you read about it and the events that led up to it, try to work out at what point things could have been turned round, and at what point disaster became inevitable. The crisis seemed to develop in ten stages.

TEN STAGES TO DISASTER

Stage 1
The day after his coronation in July 1189, King Richard I ordered that all Jews in England were to be protected. However, as soon as he left on a Crusade in March 1190 (see Lessons 3.4a and b), riots against Jews and Jewish properties broke out all over England.

Stage 2
In early March 1190, York was on fire! Houses were burning, whether accidentally or deliberately, no one knows. Using the fire as cover, a mob targeted the Jews. The family and friends of a very wealthy Jew, Baruch, who was murdered shortly after Richard I's coronation, were attacked and their houses looted. Baruch's widow and his children were murdered.

Stage 3
Josce, the leader of the Jews in York, took his family into the safety of Clifford's Tower. He urged all the Jews in York to do what he had done. About 150 of them followed his example.

Stage 4
The Tower's warden let all the Jews into the Tower, then left them alone. He must have thought they were safe because they were under the protection of the King. No one would dare attack them.

Stage 5
But the Jews were suspicious. They thought the warden might have gone off to do a deal with the mob. When he came back they wouldn't let him in and locked the doors of the Tower to keep him out.

Stage 6
The warden went straight to the sheriff, John Marshall, and complained that the Jews were cheats and liars and had tricked him. The sheriff immediately alerted the townspeople to what had happened, and called in the militia.

Stage 7
A huge crowd of townspeople besieged the Tower, threatening to force out the Jews. They besieged the Tower for days, growing angrier and more and more threatening. Then part of the Tower began to burn. The Jews realised their situation was hopeless. They knew that if they surrendered, they faced being torn limb from limb by the howling mob, or forcibly baptised as Christians or tortured. What were they to do?

Stage 8
On the night of Friday 15 March, some Jews decided to kill themselves rather than convert to Christianity. Husbands killed their wives and their children, then killed each other.

Stage 9
At daybreak, those who had survived begged the crowd to let them out. They promised to do what the mob wanted and allow themselves to be baptised as Christians. The mob agreed.

Stage 10
Never trust a mob! When the surviving Jews emerged from Clifford's Tower, blinking and a bit confused in the sudden daylight, the mob massacred them, men, women and children. Around 150 Jews died in total.

Could the outcome have been different?

2 You've read the story of the massacre. Go back to the question with which it began. Were there any points at which the situation could have been turned round so that the Jews did not die? Talk about this with a partner and reach a conclusion. Share your conclusion with the rest of your class.

Who is to blame?

3 King Richard I is furious about killings because the Jews were under his protection. He has asked you to write a report on the events of the night of Friday 15 March 1190, making it clear who you think is to blame and why.

Why were the Jews massacred in York on 16 March 1190?

Not many events have just one cause, as this story shows.

> Mrs Scott was in a hurry. She had had a row with her boss and so was late leaving work. She was feeling pretty stressed. She thought she was going to be late collecting her children from primary school. She was driving as fast as she could within the speed limits. The two front tyres on her car were worn smooth in places. To make matters worse, it was raining hard and the roads were wet and slippery with fallen leaves. Suddenly a cat ran across the road in front of her car. Mrs Scott braked hard. She missed the cat but skidded and hit a tree.

Think about it

1 **a)** Look at these reasons which could have caused Mrs Scott's accident.

- She was stressed.
- She was driving too fast.
- The car tyres were smooth in places.
- The roads were wet and slippery.
- A cat ran out in front of her.

Was there only one factor that caused the accident? Maybe the accident happened because of a combination of two or even three factors? Which two? Which three? What do you think? What does your class think?

Remember Mrs Scott and the combination of reasons for her accident as you work through the rest of this lesson.

Back to the Jews in York

Before you can work out why the Jews in York were massacred (see Lesson 3.7b), you need to know why they were there in the first place, and whether their very presence in the city could have caused stress among the other inhabitants.

By the 1170s there was a tightly knit, prosperous Jewish community in York. There were two main reasons for this.

Reason 1: The lords, gentry and monasteries in Yorkshire had an urgent need for cash, and the Jews were more than willing to lend them money. Indeed, it was only the Jews who were able to lend money at this time. They could, and did, charge high rates of interest.

Reason 2: There was an important royal castle in York, consisting of a wooden tower, Clifford's Tower, and an outer courtyard (bailey) where the Jews could go in times of danger. The Jews had been brought under the special protection of various kings of England and, at this time, they were under the protection of King Richard I. The Jews were a source of enormous wealth to the Crown, not only as money-lenders but also because the monarchs taxed them very highly.

Your turn ...

1 b) For each of these reasons why there was a Jewish community in York, write down one reason why this could have stressed the local community.

Digging deeper

Events usually have more than one cause. Do you think these facts help explain the York Massacre?

Fact 1: Richard Malebisse, the noble who led the mob attacking Clifford's Tower, was deeply in debt to the Jews.

Fact 2: Immediately after the Jews were massacred, the mob went to the cathedral. There they burned all the documents detailing the money owed to the Jews. The documents had been stored there for safekeeping.

Fact 3: The Third Crusade started in 1189. But there were many Crusader leaders who believed that they should first take revenge on the Jews living in their midst. The *New Jewish Encyclopaedia* says: 'The cry was: "Before attempting to revenge ourselves on the Muslim unbelievers, let us first revenge ourselves on the 'killers of Christ' living in our midst."' Thousands of Jews throughout Europe were massacred and whole Jewish communities were wiped out.

Prioritise!

2 Put these three facts in what you think is their order of importance in bringing about the massacre of Jews in York. Explain, in two or three sentences, why you have chosen this order.

Give an explanation

3 Why were the Jews of York massacred in March 1190? Write a paragraph in explanation, using the work you have already done in this lesson.

Remember:

- that there may be immediate causes and long-term, deep ones
- to back up what you say with evidence.

Next Lesson

3.8a

What was life like for black people in the sixteenth century?

In this lesson you will:

- find out about the lives of some of the black people who lived in Tudor England

- use information as part of an enquiry.

Key words

Blackamoor
A word used by people in Elizabethan times to describe black people.

■ *Painting from c.1650 by Aelbert Cuyp, 'Huntsmen Halted'.*

Black people in Tudor England

? *Source a is a picture of trumpet players at the court of Henry VIII. What can you see?*

Read through and look at **sources b–f**. These sources give us clues about the different experiences of black people in Tudor times in England.

■ *A painting of John Blanke and the Westminster Tournament Roll, 1511.*

c *Wealthy people in the kingdom might have one or two black servants, footmen or musicians. Some black people were slaves but there were certainly also free black people doing a variety of jobs. Queen Elizabeth I employed black musicians. The queen also had a black maidservant.*

■ *Taken from the National Archives website, 2007, Black Presence in Britain 1500–1850.*

d

We know that Catherine of Aragon landed at Deptford in 1501 with a multinational and multicultural crowd of Moors, Muslims and Jews. In Tudor times black people began to arrive in England as interpreters, sailors and servants.

■ *Taken from the National Archives website Black Settlers in Tudor Times, 2007.*

e

*Recently many **blackamoors** have been brought into this country, of which kind of people there are already here too many. Those kind of people should be sent away from this land.*

■ *Written by Elizabeth I in 1596 to mayors around the country. Elizabeth had arranged that a merchant, Casper van Senden, take 89 black people from England to swap for 89 English sailors held in Spain and Portugal.*

f

Given the lack of food in England, the Queen is upset to be told about the great number of Negroes and blackamoors which have come into England since 1588; who are looked after here, to the great annoyance of the people.

■ *Written in 1601 by Elizabeth I. Again, Elizabeth is writing to all of the mayors in the country. Clearly her suggestion of 1596 has been ignored.*

Your turn ...

1 Try to sum up each source (**b–f**). What does each one tell a historian about black people in Tudor times?

Despite having black musicians and servants, Queen Elizabeth's attitude towards black people changed in the 1590s. Here are some of the reasons why.

● In the 1590s England was going through a period of crisis: the harvests failed, bringing hunger and poverty. Elizabeth tried to blame England's black population for these problems. Many black people were Muslims, not Protestant Christians. So Elizabeth thought that they would be an easy target for blame.

● Elizabeth and the rich were worried about an increase in the number of beggars. In 1601 she passed the Poor Laws. These made strict rules about what the poor could and could not do. She tried to suggest that many black people were poor.

A historian's view

Take a look at **source g**.

g

Black people had become too securely lodged at various levels of English society to be displaced and repatriated.

■ *An explanation from a historian, James Walvin, as to why Elizabeth's letters had little impact.*

Over to you ...

2 You have Elizabeth in the hot seat. You and your group have an opportunity to put questions to her. Look again at all the sources before you draw up your list of questions. What are you going to ask about her 1596 and 1601 letters?

Now try this

3 Imagine you are the Mayor of London in 1601. You have decided to respond to Elizabeth's recent letter in **source f**. Read through all the sources one more time. In your letter you should:

● explain the different jobs that black people do

● explain why her suggestions will not work.

Remember, be polite – you want to keep your head!

In this lesson you will:

■ pass judgement on John Hawkins

■ use information and sources as part of an enquiry.

How should John Hawkins be judged?

? *Source a shows the coat of arms of John Hawkins. It was awarded to him in 1568. What does it show?*

The trial of John Hawkins

John Hawkins has gone down in history as the 'father of the slave trade'. He was born in 1532 and spent most of his life at sea, where he died 1595. However, Hawkins was not just a slave trader. In his life he did many things and it is important to give him a fair hearing. Below are several exhibits that we will use in the trial of John Hawkins. There is a range of charges against him. You should consider the evidence before choosing one charge you think best suits Hawkins.

The charges

There are three possible charges that you can bring against John Hawkins.

Charge 1: Hawkins was the 'father of the slave trade'.

Charge 2: Hawkins was involved in the slave trade but was not alone.

Charge 3: There is no case to answer: slavery was normal for the time.

Look at the evidence

1 Read through **A–G** in pairs or groups.

a) Which evidence supports which charge? After someone in your group has read out or described the evidence, discuss it before making your decision.

b) Once you have read through all the evidence, decide as a group which charge you will bring against Hawkins.

■ *John Hawkins's coat-of-arms, 1568.*

A

In 1555 London trader John Lok brought five slaves from Guinea to England. He was followed by another London trader, William Towerson, who brought African slaves to England in 1556 and 1557.

B

Pirates from North Africa (known as Barbary Pirates) seized 466 British ships between 1609 and 1616 and sold their sailors into slavery. They even raided Cornish villages such as Mousehole and took their inhabitants away to be slaves. In the late 1500s there were around 35,000 European slaves held in North Africa.

C

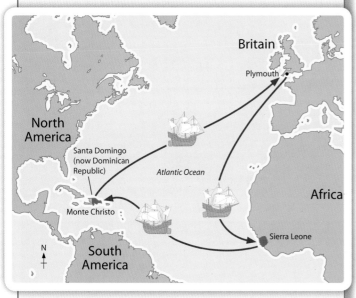

■ *A map showing the route of Hawkins' first adventure.*

D

The first Europeans to trade in African slaves were the Portuguese in the sixteenth century. From 1540 they seized or bought Africans and took them across the Atlantic to work in Brazil on the sugar plantations. Some of the Africans were sold to the Portuguese by African traders.

E

In 1562 Hawkins sailed in the *Salomon* down the Guinea coast and took 300 Africans as slaves. At Sierra Leone he seized a ship with another 500 Africans on board. He then sailed to the Dominican Republic in the West Indies, where he sold 125 slaves for around £30 each to the owners of sugar and tobacco plantations.

F

John Hawkins set the pattern for the Atlantic slave trade that was to carry millions of Africans into slavery over the next 270 years. But Hawkins was not alone in being involved in slavery. Many rich people, including Queen Elizabeth I, backed him. In 1564 the queen lent Hawkins her ship, the *Jesus of Lubeck*, to use to capture African slaves.

G

Hawkins should not be remembered just for starting the slave trade. He was a Member of Parliament and, from 1573, he reorganised the English Navy introducing smaller and faster warships. In 1588 he played a major part in the defeat of the Spanish Armada.

Consider the evidence

2 Decide on the charges to be brought against John Hawkins. Prepare a statement for either the defence or the prosecution in this case. Make sure you use the evidence from these pages to support your statement.

In conclusion ...

3 Now you have to make two judgements.
   a) **The Historian:** which verdict do you, as a historian using the exhibits, think is the right one for Hawkins?
   b) **The Elizabethan:** which verdict do you think would be decided by someone living at the same time as Hawkins?

   Do the charges differ and, if so, why?

In this lesson you will:

- discover about the life and adventures of Marco Polo

- use evidence in an enquiry.

The adventures of Marco Polo

In 1298, a man called Rustichello from Pisa, in Italy, found himself sharing a prison cell with Marco Polo. They had been captured in a sea raid by sailors from Genoa. As they sat in their prison cell, Marco began to tell Rustichello stories of his travels in China. Rustichello thought that Marco's stories were so amazing, he began to write them down. When they were released from prison, Rustichello put these stories together into a book, *The Travels of Marco Polo*.

? *Here are some pictures inspired by* **The Travels of Marco Polo.** *What can you see?*

- *Three images taken from* Les Livres du Graunt Caam *(fifteenth century).*

Marco Polo was clearly quite an amazing person.
Here are some details about his life.

Factfile

EARLY LIFE

Name

Marco Polo

Born

1254 in Venice

Father

Niccolo Polo, a rich merchant

Places visited as a child

Russia and China

SECOND JOURNEY ABROAD

Date of departure

1271

Places visited

See map over the page

Aim of visit

To bring a message from the Pope in Rome to the Chinese ruler Kublai Khan, known as the Great Khan

Jobs

Ambassador and messenger for the Great Khan

DESCRIPTIONS FROM HIS TRAVELS

Tibet

'Is full of bamboo forests but also the greatest robbers in the world.'

Pagan

'The king's grave is covered by two towers: one made of silver, the other gold.'

Yangtze River

'Was so wide it looked like the sea.'

India

'Here divers fish for pearls.'

Ceylon

'The biggest ruby in the world glowed red like fire.'

Date returned home

1295

1 Marco Polo forgot to tell his family at home how he was getting on in China. Now is your chance to change that.

Design a postcard that you will fill in and send to Venice. On one side, draw some of the amazing images that Marco Polo saw and described. On the other, try to sum up some of your experiences.

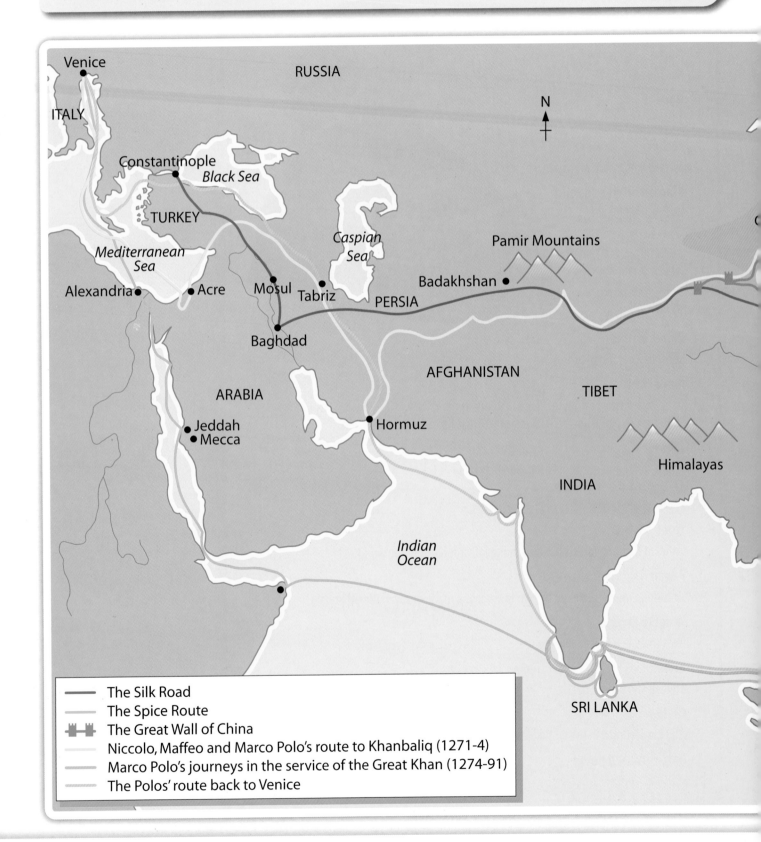

Venice

RUSSIA

ITALY

N

Constantinople
Black Sea

TURKEY

Caspian Sea

Pamir Mountains

Mediterranean Sea

Badakhshan

Alexandria   Acre   Mosul   Tabriz   PERSIA

Baghdad

AFGHANISTAN

TIBET

ARABIA

Jeddah
Mecca

Hormuz

Himalayas

INDIA

Indian Ocean

SRI LANKA

— The Silk Road
— The Spice Route
⊞ The Great Wall of China
— Niccolo, Maffeo and Marco Polo's route to Khanbaliq (1271-4)
— Marco Polo's journeys in the service of the Great Khan (1274-91)
--- The Polos' route back to Venice

The factfile page 171 and the map will give you some idea of the amazing adventures enjoyed by Marco Polo. But when Marco Polo, his father and uncle arrived home in Venice, their family were astonished to see them. They had been away for 24 years. The family had plenty of questions to ask them!

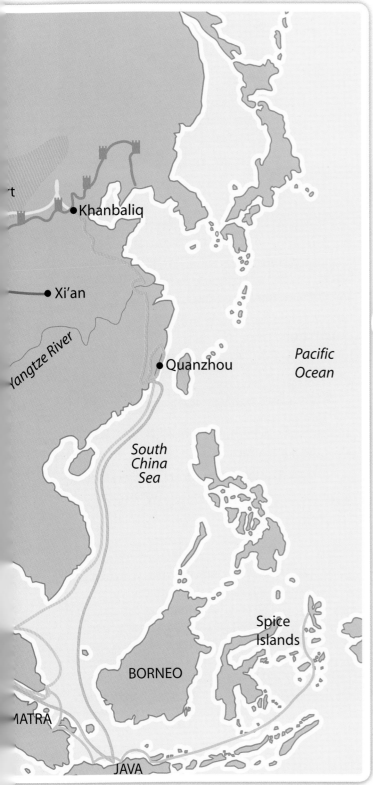

Over to you ...

2 Come up with five questions Marco Polo's family might have asked him and the answers he might have given.

Write the story

3 Using the factfile and the map, prepare a 300-word summary of Marco Polo's life to read to his family.

History detective

Marco Polo wasn't the only medieval explorer. Which European explorers are these?

- He had ships called the *Pinta*, the *Nina* and the *Santa Maria*.
- He was the first to sail round the Cape of Good Hope, and across the Indian Ocean to Calicut.
- He was the first to round Cape Horn.
- He failed to find a north-west passage to India but instead claimed North America for Britain.
- He had the straits at the tip of South America named after him.
- He was sponsored by the joint monarchs of Spain, Ferdinand and Isabella, to find a sea route to India by sailing west.
- He was the first to sail right round the world.
- He thought he had reached India, so called the land he discovered the West Indies.

In this lesson you will:

- use the sources to find out what Francis Drake was like as a sea captain

- work out whether or not you would have liked to have sailed with him.

Francis Drake

Francis Drake lived from c.1540 to 1596. To the Spanish he was a pirate and a criminal. He was also a slave trader, a politician and navigator. He was a hero to the English when he was second in command of the fleet that defeated the Spanish Armada in 1588.

Look closely at **source a**.
Do you trust this man?

■ Portrait from 1583, painted when Francis Drake was 43 years old.

Use your eyes!

1 Look at **source a**.

a) What words would you use to describe Francis Drake – just by looking at this portrait? Calm? Shy? Brave? Determined? Gentle? Nasty? Wicked?

Write a sentence to say why you have chosen the words you have, e.g.:

I think Francis Drake looks _____ because …

b) Sometimes we make decisions based on our first impression of someone. Would you trust Francis Drake? You're going to have to if you sail with him!

Write a sentence to say whether you would or not:

I would / would not trust Francis Drake because …

Circumnavigating the world, 1577–1580

Francis Drake's most famous voyage was when he sailed right round the world. A lot of accounts written by those who sailed with him have survived, so we can work out what sort of a captain he was and what it would have been like to have sailed with him.

As we can see from **sources b–d**, at the start of the journeys hardly anyone knew where they were going.

They left Plymouth towards the end of December and John Drake went in the Captain's ship, serving him as a page. John understood that when they left England there were not two men in the fleet who knew where they were going. Once the crew found out what was happening, there was trouble! A group of them, led by Thomas Doughty, mutinied.

Thomas Doughty, one of the gentlemen who was with him, said to Francis Drake: 'We have been a long while in this strait and you have placed all of us, who follow or serve you, in danger of death. It would therefore be wise of you to give the order that we return to the north sea, where we are certain to capture prizes. We must give up trying to make new discoveries.' Drake dealt with the situation swiftly. He had the man beheaded in front of all the crew! Although he was strict with his men, Drake seems to have been well liked by them.

■ *Testimonies of Francisco de Zarate, 1579, from* New Light on Drake: A Collection of Documents Relating to His Voyage of Circumnavigation 1577–1580.

d

All his crew are of an age for warfare and take pains to keep their weapons clean. He treats them with affection and they treat him with respect. He takes advice from no one, but enjoys hearing what his men have to say and then issues his orders. He has no favourites. All the men he carries with him receive wages. He shows them great favour but punishes the least fault.

■ *Testimony of Francisco de Zarate, 1579, from* New Light on Drake: A Collection of Documents Relating to His Voyage of Circumnavigation 1577–1580.

Drake lived in style on his ship, as **sources e** and **f** show.

e

He is served on silver dishes with gold borders and gilded garlands, which show his coat of arms. He carried all possible dainties and perfumed waters. He said that many of them had been given to him by the queen. During their round-the-world voyage, Drake and his crew attacked Spanish ships and ports, collecting treasures for themselves.

■ *Testimony of Nuno da Silva, 1579, from* New Light on Drake: A Collection of Documents Relating to His Voyage of Circumnavigation 1577–1580.

f

On 27 February, at night, Drake captured another ship bound for Panama and laden with stuff for the King of Spain. He took two thousand bags and other things and with 40 bars of silver and gold. And because a sailor secretly took one bar of gold, Drake had him hanged.

■ *Testimony of Nuno da Silva, 1579, from* New Light on Drake: A Collection of Documents Relating to His Voyage of Circumnavigation 1577–1580.

The voyage was worth it though: Drake returned to London with almost five tons of treasure! He was also authorised to secretly take a large amount for himself and his crew.

History detective

- How did sailors work out how fast they were going?
- What did sailors eat when fresh food ran out?
- What was an astrolabe used for?
- What was a cross-staff used for?
- What is dead reckoning?
- What is scurvy?
- Why did some captains not tell their crew where they were going or how long they would be at sea?

What do you think of Drake now?

2 a) What words would you use to describe Francis Drake now? Brave? Arrogant? Cruel? Fair? Think about it, and talk to the person next to you. Do you have the same opinion? If not, why not? Are you giving different sources greater importance?

b) When Francis Drake arrived back in London after sailing around the world, Queen Elizabeth visited his ship and knighted him. Does this mean she approved of what he had done?

In conclusion ...

3 If you had been given the chance, would you have set out on his round-the-world journey with Francis Drake? Use as many sources as you can to support your view.

Back to the start

You've found out about at least two European explorers. You know that sea voyages at this time were difficult and dangerous. Why, then, did people set out to explore the world?

Next Lesson

Why did people move around in the Middle Ages?

In this unit you have been working through enquiries that have looked at people on the move. Sometimes they haven't gone far – perhaps to the nearest market; others have left all they own and know, and have gone to live in a foreign land; some have pushed at the borders of empire, expanding and extending it; and others have travelled around the world.

Look at these maps.

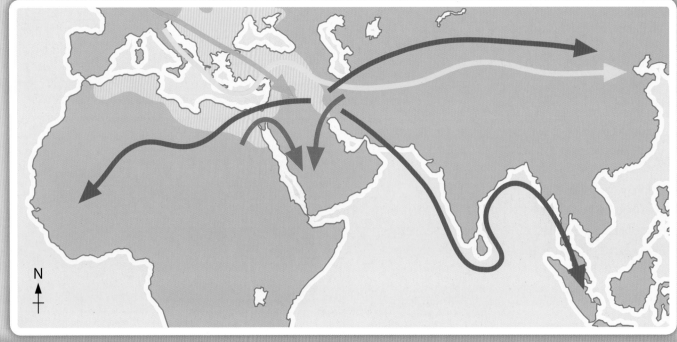

Your turn ...

1 Working in groups of three to four, study one of these maps. Look back through this unit and work out which groups of travellers would have moved along the arrows on your map.

Now join with other groups working on the same map and share your ideas.

PUSH

Some people travelled because they had to. There may have been small, personal reasons such as the need to earn money to put food on the table. There may have been large, perhaps national, reasons like King Edward I's decision to expel all Jews from England. These are often called the 'push' factors.

Push and pull factors

As you have seen, some people were on the move in the Middle Ages. But why?

PULL

Then there are the 'pull' factors. What was it that was attractive at the other end of the journey? Was it the chance to sell cheese in the local market? To trade silks in the Far East? To take Jerusalem from the Muslims? Or the excitement of sailing into the unknown?

Over to You ...

2 Get back in your original groups. For each group of travellers on your map, sort out whether there was a push factor, a pull factor, or both.

Pulling it all together

3 What links all the people on your map? Think of ways in which you can show your class how the people on your map were linked. A PowerPoint presentation? A poster? Imaginary interviews with them? And do it!

Assessment 1

Did travelling in England improve between 1285–1450?

Study the sources below and answer the questions that follow.

- The royal ladies' travelling coach, taken from the Luttrell Psalter, c.1340

- Written by King Edward I to the Prior and people of Dunstable in 1285.

We have learned that the high roads that stretch through Dunstable are so broken up by the frequent passage of carts, that dangerous injuries threaten those using the roads. We therefore command each one of you according to his means [money] to fill in and mend the roads.

- Extract from the Statute of Westminster, passed by King Edward I and parliament in 1285.

Highways leading from one market town to another shall be widened where there are bushes or ditches, so that there shall be no bushes or ditches for a man to hide in to do hurt to travellers within 200 feet of the road.

1 a) Source a is a picture from the time of medieval people travelling. What can you tell from this picture about travel in medieval England?

  b) Why do you think Edward I was so concerned that travellers should be safe?

  c) Do **sources b** and **c** prove that the roads in England were kept in good condition?

- Extract from the records of Parliament, 1450. It gives an account of the disaster that hit a traveller between Northampton and London.

Some 160 persons and more, all dressed as if for war with light helmets, long swords and other weapons, hid under a large hedge near the highway. They lay in wait for William Tresham from midnight to the hour of six, at which time William appeared. They attacked him and struck him through his body and foot. They gave him more deadly wounds and cut his throat. He died.

2 d) Does **source d** mean that people hadn't taken any notice of what parliament and King Edward I ordered in **source c**?

  e) Use these four sources and your own knowledge to answer the question: Did travelling in England improve between 1285–1450?

How are you going to set about a task like this?

1 **a)** Don't just **describe** what you can see.
Think about what you can see. What conclusions can you draw? For example, if there was a black person in the carriage you could just write: 'There is a black person in the carriage.' But if you thought about it for a bit, you might then write: 'This means that there were black people in England at that time and that they travelled in rich looking carriages.' Inferences get more marks than descriptions!

b) Let's look at **source b** first. What did the king want the Prior and people of Dunstable to do? And what does this tell you about the state of the roads? Look now at **source c**. An order is a sort of rule, so you must think backwards from this. What was it the king and parliament were trying to stop? **Think!** What would pushing the undergrowth, trees and bushes back from the sides of the road prevent? Next think about why the king and parliament would want to prevent this happening.

c) Very rarely can two sources prove anything. They might be from different times, different parts of the same country or even from different countries. But they can give you some sort of clue about what is happening. Read them both carefully and think about what **inferences** you can make. Remember to look at who wrote them and what the significance of this could be. Looking at two or more sources to answer a question is called **cross-referencing**.

d) **Think!** A king may have ordered something nearly 200 years earlier and his orders may have been carried out then. But is there any reason to suppose his orders will have been carried out in 1450? If not, why did things get worse – and did they get worse everywhere?

e) Use your knowledge as well as the sources. Look back to enquiries 3a–3b to remind yourself what was happening. How far do the sources back up what you know, and how far do they say something else? Remember the sources may be unreliable and may, in any case, only give you a snapshot in time and of a particular place. So while things may be bad, or good, for a person or a place, that doesn't necessarily mean they are bad or good everywhere.

How will your work be marked? Have you:

Level 4
Described the problems involved in travelling, showing that you understand that there were differences within the time period?

Identified ways in which travelling changed between 1285 and 1450 and why it changed?

Used the right sort of information to answer the question? Written in clear sentences using the right dates and historical words?

Level 5
Shown that you understand that the problems involved in travelling differed from time to time and place to place?

Described ways in which travelling improved between 1285 and 1450, and suggested why it improved?

Selected information that best answers the question in a sensible, structured way?

Level 6
Begun to sort out why the problems involved in travelling might have differed from time to time and place to place?

Explained the ways in which travelling improved between 1285 and 1540, and why these improvements occurred?

Selected and organised relevant information that best answers the question?

Why did people make long journeys?

? *You have been asked to set up an exhibition in your local library. The exhibition is to be called: 'Why did medieval people make long journeys?' Unfortunately, there isn't much space. You can only select six items for the exhibition. For each item you have selected, you will have to write a brief explanation as to why it is especially good at showing why medieval people took long journeys.*

Lots of ideas are probably swirling around in your head as to which six items you are going to choose. These are probably some of them …

How are you going to set about a task like this?

Here are some handy hints!

- Look through Unit 3 and make a quick note of which items might be good to use.

- Then start sorting through your large collection to make a smaller one.

- Each item you choose should show something different about why medieval people went on long journeys. You might, for example, choose a Crusader's horse and Marco Polo's ship as showing that Crusaders travelled to keep Jerusalem Christian and Marco Polo travelled for adventure and trade.

- Choose different sorts of items in order to make the exhibition interesting for the public who will be coming along to look at it. For example, don't choose all animals, or all written documents or all artefacts. Have a mixture.

- Work out what you are going to say about each item. Remember you have to explain why you have chosen it and what it shows about the reasons medieval people travelled far. Don't write a lot – just something sharp and to the point.

How are you going to display your items?

You could display your items in a number of different ways. Here are some suggestions. You can probably think of more.

- You could scan the items, add your own words and create a PowerPoint presentation.

- You could photocopy or scan the items and paste them onto cards, add your own words to each item and set them up as a mini-exhibition on a table, desk, wall or in your file.

- You could make a large poster showing the items and explanations.

How will your work be marked?
Have you:

Level 4
Selected six items and described each one?

Identified some of the reasons why people made long journeys?

Used the right sort of information to complete this task? Written in clear sentences using the right dates and historical words?

Level 5
Selected six items and explained why each is especially good at showing why medieval people made long journeys?

Linked together some of the reasons why people made long journeys?

Selected information that best answers the question in a sensible, structured way?

Level 6
Selected six items, each one of which show a different reason why medieval people made long journeys and explained this?

Explained the links between the reasons why people made long journeys?

Selected and organised relevant information to complete this task?

Use this section to remind yourself of some important historical skills. These hints will be useful as you complete the tasks and activities in this book.

Being a historian

These are some of the things that a historian does.

- Tells the story of the past.
- Explains why things happened and the consequences.
- Shows that some things change while others stay the same.
- Identifies why certain events and people are important.
- Works as a detective using evidence.
- Communicates about the past.

Throughout this book you will have the chance to practise and improve all of these skills. First, read through the descriptions below to find out what kind of historian are you.

Level 4

You can:

- tell the story of the past quite well
- give some reasons why events happen
- describe how some things have changed but others stay the same
- show how the past can be looked at in different ways
- use evidence to explain the past
- use the right words to explain the past.

Level 5

You can:

- tell the story of the past
- begin to explain why things happen
- explain how some things change while others stay the same
- begin to explain why some events and people are really important
- begin to ask questions of evidence
- use the right information to explain the past.

Level 6

You can:

- tell and explain the story of the past
- begin to explain how causes link together
- explain in detail why some things change and others stay the same
- ask questions why some people or events are more important than others
- decide which evidence is useful
- use the right information and organise ideas clearly.

Evaluating a source

Evaluating a source means looking at it (or reading it) carefully and asking questions about it so that you can decide how valuable it is to a historian. Whatever the source, whether it's a diary or a letter, a photograph or a painting, you need to think about its nature (what it is), its origin (when and where it comes from, who it is by) and its purpose (why it was made). Use the 5xW rule to help you remember key questions to ask about the nature, origin and purpose of a source.

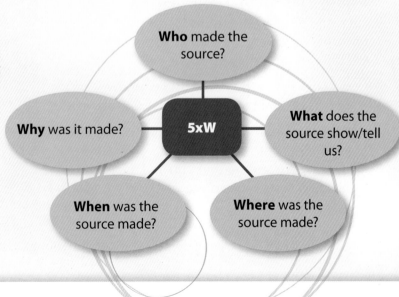

Who made the source?

What does the source show/tell us?

5xW

Why was it made?

Where was the source made?

When was the source made?

Exploding a picture

Pictures, especially paintings, are not always what they seem. Sometimes they tell us far more than the artist intended them to. Sometimes they lead us to ask more and more questions so that the picture turns into a puzzle.

Look at this picture. You first saw it in Lesson 2.9a, when you were finding out about how the Tudors had fun. But there's more to it than that!

First think about the artist. This is called looking at the provenance or origin of the painting. Remember the **5×W** rule!

- Who painted the picture?
- When did they paint it?
- Was he (or she) there at the time?
- Were they in a good position to know what was going on, or did they make it up afterwards?

- Why did he (or she) paint the picture?
- Did someone pay them to do it?
- Were they trying to make a particular point?

You won't find answers to all these questions for every picture you look at, but you need to bear them in mind and answer the ones you can.

Now look at the picture itself. It is called 'A Wedding at Bermondsey'.

- What can you see that tells you that this is a wedding celebration?
- Can you spot people dancing? Musicians? Guests? Food being prepared?
- Are there two people who might be the married couple?

This is what the artist set out to show.

There are other things in the painting that the artist did not set out to show but which tell us a lot about, in this case, Tudor times. This is called 'unwitting testimony'. Look carefully at the painting.

- What does it tell you about the clothes worn by adults?
- The clothes worn by children?
- Musical instruments?
- Cooking?

- Buildings?
- The way guests got to the wedding?

Bermondsey is now, and was then, part of London. So what can you tell about Tudor London from the painting?

Finally check what you can see in the painting against what you know about life in Tudor England.

Do you think this painting can be considered reliable evidence of a Tudor wedding? **Why? Why not?**

1 Now find another painting in this book.

Use the provenance to work out whether or not it is likely to be reliable evidence of what it illustrates.

Use the title and the content to describe what the artist set out to show.

Look behind what the artist set out to show to think about what else you can find out.

Unpacking a written source

Remember the **5xW** rule! This applies as much to written sources as it does to pictures and paintings.

Read through this source. (You first came across it in Lesson 1.8a when you were deciding whether or not Richard III killed his nephews Edward and Richard.)

source

After his coronation in July 1483, King Richard decided that he must kill his nephews. This was because as long as they were alive, no one would believe him to be the true king. Sir James Tyrell agreed to plan the murder. He decided that the princes should be murdered in their beds. He chose Miles Forest and John Dighton to do the deed. The two men pressed feather beds and pillows hard on the children's faces until they stopped breathing. The story is well known to be true because Sir James Tyrell confessed to it when he was imprisoned in the Tower in 1502.

■ *From Sir Thomas More's* The History of King Richard III, *written in 1513.*

Using a written source

2 Apply the **5xW** rule to this source to help you answer this question:
How useful is this source to a historian trying to find out whether or not King Richard III killed the princes in the Tower?

What else do I need to think about?

In order to answer a question like the one in **task 2** fully, you will need to think about each of the following.

Bias

A source might be biased. This means that it gives you an argument or an opinion from one person's point of view and is not balanced. But take care. Just because a person may be biased about a particular event or individual doesn't mean that everything he or she writes or draws is automatically biased too.

Reliability

Once you have checked out the **5xW** rule you will be able to decide whether or not a source tells you accurately about the person, event or time it is describing.

Usefulness

Thinking about the **5xWs**, **reliability** and **bias** will lead you to consider usefulness (sometimes called utility). When you are thinking about whether a source is useful, you'll need to ask: 'Useful for what?' Useful for wrapping up your fish and chips? Perhaps not! Useful for finding out whether John was a bad king? Maybe!

Remember, every source is useful at some time and for something.

- Biased sources are useful because they tell you a lot about the person who wrote, drew or painted them.
- Reliable sources are useful because you can count on them to be telling you accurately about the time, person or event.

Using what you know

3 Apply **bias**, **reliability** and **usefulness** to what Sir Thomas More had to say about the princes in the Tower (see task 1b). You should now have a full answer to the question: *How useful is this source to a historian trying to find out whether or not King Richard III killed the princes in the Tower?*

Communicating about the past

All historians need to be able to communicate their ideas.
This can be done in two ways:

- using writing
- verbally.

Whichever way you communicate your ideas, you should do the following.

- **Plan:** map out your work before you start.
- **Structure:** every piece of work should be clearly structured including the use of an introduction and a conclusion.
- **(Use) Evidence:** all ideas should be backed up with accurate information.

The plan

A good plan is the secret to success. It will help you to work out what you want to say before you start.

Your plan should have two parts to it:

- the main points that you are going to make
- what is to be put in each paragraph/section.

You can set out your plan in a number of ways. For example, you might want to use a diagram.

Here is an example plan for the question: *How successful was William I's reign?*

Successful: All opposition was crushed.

Successful: Norman rule set up with the building of castles

Successful: Domesday Book

MAIN POINTS

Successful: Introduction of the feudal system

Not successful: Poor relations with the English

Structure

Think about your paragraph/section running order.

Introduction: writing out the main points from the plan

1 Crushing opposition
2 Castle building
3 The Feudal System
4 Administration and the Domesday book
5 Relations with the English

Conclusion: sum up your main points

Using evidence

When you make a point, make sure you back it up with evidence. Each paragraph or section should include the following.

- **Point:** make your point.
- **Evidence:** back up your point with evidence from sources or your own knowledge.
- **Explanation:** explain why you have chosen that piece of evidence.

Opposite is an example of a paragraph.

Point   Evidence   Explanation

William's reign was successful because he was able to control the country by building castles. Motte and bailey castles were built quickly. The castles housed soldiers as well as the new Norman rulers. They were very difficult to attack. In the first ten years of his reign William built castles in many towns including Rochester, Hastings and Dover.

Put it into practice

4 d) Explain why people went on the First Crusade.

- What are the main points for your plan?
- What is your paragraph/section running order?

Glossary

Abbot
Head monk in an abbey.

Archaeologist
Someone who is specially trained to uncover ruins of old buildings and towns. They find everyday objects and help us to build up a picture of how people lived in the past.

Baron
An important landowner who provided men to fight for the king if necessary.

Blackamoor
A word used by people in Elizabethan times to describe black people.

Burgess
An important person in a town.

Chancellor
The king's chief minister and adviser.

Chronicle
A written record of events. It was very important in a time without newspapers.

Crusade
A Christian military expedition made with the aim of recovering Jerusalem from the Muslims.

Customs duties
A tax paid to the government on some goods when they left the country, were brought into the country, and sometimes on both movements of goods.

Enclose common land
Put fences and hedges around land that previously everyone could use.

Exchequer
Part of the government responsible for collecting money.

Freeman
Man who was free to leave his lord's lands, and who could live and work wherever he wanted. Some peasants were freemen, others were slaves.

Great Council
Meeting of all the most powerful lords in the country to advise the king on what he should do.

Heresy
When people have an opinion or belief that goes against the views of the Church.

Holy Land
The region on the eastern shore of the Mediterranean which Christians, Jews and Muslims all treat as important to their religions.

Idolater
A person who does not worship a single God. They worship an idol or idols instead.

Infidel
The name given to someone of a different religion from one's own.

Interest rates
The sum or rate charged for borrowing money.

Jury
Group of twelve people who have to decide if someone is guilty or not guilty of the crime for which they have been accused.

Ka'bah
The building towards which Muslims face five times every day in prayer.

Mark
Weight of gold or silver equal to 226.8 grams.

Martyr
Person who dies for their faith.

Mass
The most important part of a Catholic church service, where the priest blesses bread and wine and offers them to God. Believers think that at this point the bread and wine become the body and blood of God's son, Jesus Christ.

Merchant
Someone who buys and sells goods, but does not make them.

New World
The Americas, newly discovered by Spain.

Parchment
Thin material made from the skin of an animal, used for writing on.

Parish
England was divided into areas called 'parishes'. Each parish had a church and a priest, although sometimes parishes had to share a priest.

Parliament
A meeting of the king's advisers to grant him money, discuss problems and make laws. The name comes from the French word *parler*, which means 'to talk'.

Pauper
A person who is receiving poor relief.

Poll Tax
A tax paid by every adult in the country in the Middle Ages. Everyone had to pay the same amount of money.

Poor relief
Help given to poor people by the parish so they could survive.

Prior
Head monk in a priory.

Psalter
A book of psalms, which are holy songs and hymns from the Bible.

Purgatory
A place between heaven and hell where Catholics believe people's souls stay until all their sins have gone.

Reconstruct
Build or draw something to show how it might have been, using evidence from archaeologists.

Relic
Part of a saint, like a bone or lock of hair.

Repentance
Showing sorrow for something you have done in the past.

Sanctuary
A place of safety, usually a church or religious establishment.

Shrine
A holy place, usually associated with an important religious person.

Siege
Attempt to force a town or a castle to surrender by surrounding it.

Sorcery
A type of magic in which spirits, especially evil ones, are used to make things happen.

Templar
A member of a religious military order founded in Jerusalem about 1118.

Vagrant
A wandering beggar.

Index